MIDSUMMER

Llewellyn's Sabbat Essentials

MIDSUMMER

Rituals, Recipes & Lore for Litha

Llewellyn Publications
Woodbury, Minnesota

FIRST EDITION
Fifteenth Printing, 2023

Book design by Donna Burch-Brown
Cover art: iStockphoto.com/18232461/©Electric_Crayon,
         iStockphoto.com/22042443/©Shlapak_Liliya,
         iStockphoto.com/18688862/©sergwsq
         iStockphoto.com/15419951/©pinkcoala
Cover design: Kevin R. Brown
Interior illustrations: Mickie Mueller

Llewellyn Publications is a registered trademark of Llewellyn Worldwide Ltd.

Library of Congress Cataloging-in-Publication Data
Blake, Deborah, 1960–
 Midsummer : rituals, recipes, and lore for Litha / by Deborah Blake. — First Edition.
   pages   cm. — (Llewellyn's sabbat essentials ; #3)
 Includes bibliographical references and index.
 ISBN 978-0-7387-4182-6
1. Midsummer. I. Title.
 BF1572.M53 B53 2015
 299'.94—dc23

                                                              2014035548

Llewellyn Publications
A Division of Llewellyn Worldwide Ltd.
2143 Wooddale Drive
Woodbury, MN 55125-2989
www.llewellyn.com

Printed in the United States of America

Contents

beginnings, birth, renewal, rejuvenation, balance, fertility, change

strength, vernal equinox, sun enters Aries, Libra in the Sou

Green Man, Amalthea, Aphrodite, Blodeuwedd, Eostre, Eo

Flora, Freya, Gaia, Guinevere, Persephone, Libera, Ma

pet, Umaj, Vila, Aengus MacOg, Cernunnos, Herma, The

ema, Mabon Osiris, Pan, Thor, abundance, growth, health, eac

l healing, patience, understanding, virtue, spring, honor, contentme

hic abilities, spiritual truth, intuition, receptivity, love, inner sel

rovement, spiritual awareness, purification, childhood, innocence,

ty, creativity, communication, concentration, divination, harmon

bilities, prosperity, attraction, blessings, happiness, luck, money,

, guidance, visions, insight, family, wishes, celebrating life cyc

ndship, courage, attracts love, honesty, good health, emotions,

improvement, influence, motivation, peace, rebirth, self preservat

mine power, freedom, optimism, new beginnings, vernal equinox

reation, sun, apple blossom, columbine, crocus, daffodil, daisy,

y, honeysuckle, jasmine, jonquil, lilac, narcissus, orange blossom,

rose, rose, the fool, the magician, the priestess, justice, the star

gathering, growth, abbundance, eggs, seeds, honey, dill, asparag

LLEWELLYN'S SABBAT ESSENTIALS

$\mathcal{L}$LEWELLYN'S SABBAT ESSENTIALS provides instruction and inspiration for honoring each of the modern witch's sabbats. Packed with spells, rituals, meditations, history, lore, invocations, divination, recipes, crafts, and more, each book in this eight-volume series explores both the old and new ways of celebrating the seasonal rites that act as cornerstones in the witch's year.

There are eight sabbats, or holidays, celebrated by Wiccans and many other Neopagans (modern Pagans) today. Together, these eight sacred days make up what's known as the Wheel of the Year, or the sabbat cycle, with each sabbat corresponding to an important turning point in nature's annual journey through the seasons.

Devoting our attention to the Wheel of the Year allows us to better attune ourselves to the energetic cycles of nature and listen to what each season is whispering (or shouting!) to us, rather than working against the natural tides. What better time to start new projects than as the earth reawakens after a long winter, and suddenly everything is blooming and growing and shooting up out of the ground again? And what better time to meditate and plan ahead than during the introspective slumber of winter? With Llewellyn's Sabbat Essentials, you'll learn how to focus on the spiritual aspects of the Wheel of the Year, how to move through it and with it in harmony, and how to celebrate your own ongoing growth and achievements. This may be your first book on Wicca, Witchcraft, or Paganism, or your newest addition to a bookcase or e-reader already crammed with magickal wisdom. In either case, we hope you will find something of value here to take with you on your journey.

Take a Trip Through the Wheel of the Year

The eight sabbats each mark an important point in nature's annual cycles. They are depicted as eight evenly spaced spokes on a wheel representing the year as a whole; the dates on which they fall are nearly evenly spaced on the calendar, as well.

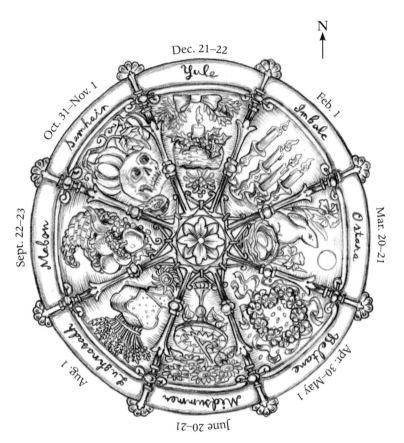

N

Dec. 21–22

Yule

Feb. 1

Imbolc

Oct. 31–Nov. 1

Samhain

Mar. 20–21

Ostara

Sept. 22–23

Mabon

Apr. 30–May 1

Beltane

Aug. 1

Lughnasadh

Midsummer

June 20–21

Wheel of the Year—Northern Hemisphere
(All solstice and equinox dates are approximate,
and one should consult an almanac or a calendar
to find the correct dates each year.)

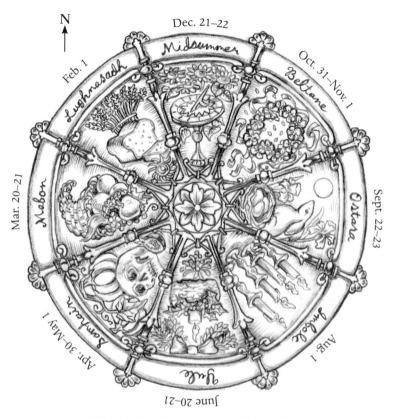

N

Dec. 21–22

Midsummer

Feb. 1

Oct. 31–Nov. 1

Lughnasadh

Beltane

Mar. 20–21

Mabon

Ostara

Sept. 22–23

Apr. 30–May 1

Samhain

Imbolc

Aug. 1

Yule

June 20–21

Wheel of the Year—Southern Hemisphere

The wheel is comprised of two groups of four holidays each. There are four solar festivals relating to the sun's position in the sky, dividing the year into quarters: the Spring Equinox, the Summer Solstice, the Fall Equinox, and the Winter Solstice, all of which are dated astronomically and thus vary slightly from year to year. Falling in between these quarter days are the cross-quarter holidays, or fire festivals: Imbolc, Beltane, Lughnasadh, and Samhain. The quarters are sometimes called the Lesser Sabbats and the cross-quarters the Greater Sabbats, although neither cycle is "superior" to the other. In the Southern Hemisphere, seasons are opposite those in the north, and the sabbats are consequently celebrated at different times.

While the book you are holding only focuses on Midsummer, it can be helpful to know how it fits in with the cycle as a whole.

The Winter Solstice, also called Yule or Midwinter, occurs when nighttime has reached its maximum length; after the solstice, the length of the days will begin to increase. Though the cold darkness is upon us, there is a promise of brighter days to come. In Wiccan lore, this is the time when the young solar god is born. In some Neopagan traditions, this is when the Holly King is destined to lose the battle to his lighter aspect, the Oak King. Candles are lit, feasts are enjoyed, and evergreen foliage is brought in the house as a reminder that, despite the harshness of winter, light and life have endured.

At Imbolc (also spelled Imbolg), the ground is just starting to thaw, signaling that it's time to start preparing the fields for the approaching sowing season. We begin to awaken from our months of introspection and start to sort out what we have learned over that time, while also taking the first steps to make plans for our future. Some Wiccans also bless candles at Imbolc, another symbolic way of coaxing along the now perceptibly stronger light.

On the Spring Equinox, also known as Ostara, night and day are again equal in length, and following this, the days will grow longer than the nights. The Spring Equinox is a time of renewal, a time to plant seeds as the earth once again comes to life. We decorate eggs as a symbol of hope, life, and fertility, and we perform rituals to energize ourselves so that we can find the power and passion to live and grow.

In agricultural societies, Beltane marked the start of the summer season. Livestock were led out to graze in abundant pastures and trees burst into beautiful and fragrant blossom. Rituals were performed to protect crops, livestock, and people. Fires were lit and offerings were made in the hopes of gaining divine protection. In Wiccan mythos, the young god impregnates the young goddess. We all have something we want to harvest by the end of the year—plans we are determined to realize—and Beltane is a great time to enthusiastically get that process in full swing.

The Summer Solstice is the longest day of the year. It's also called Litha, or Midsummer. Solar energies are at their apex, and the power of nature is at its height. In Wiccan lore, it's the time when the solar god's power is at its greatest (so, paradoxically, his power must now start to decrease), having impregnated the maiden goddess, who then transforms into the earth mother. In some Neopagan traditions, this is when the Holly King once again battles his lighter aspect, this time vanquishing the Oak King. It's generally a time of great merriment and celebration.

At Lughnasadh, the major harvest of the summer has ripened. Celebrations are held, games are played, gratitude is expressed, and feasts are enjoyed. Also known as Lammas, this is the time we celebrate the first harvest—whether that means the first of our garden crops or the first of our plans that have come to fruition. To celebrate the grain harvest, bread is often baked on this day.

The Autumn Equinox, also called Mabon, marks another important seasonal change and a second harvest. The sun shines equally on both hemispheres, and the lengths of night and day are equal. After this point, the nights will again be longer than the days. In connection with the harvest, the day is celebrated as a festival of sacrifice and of the dying god, and tribute is paid to the sun and the fertile earth.

To the Celtic people, Samhain marked the start of the winter season. It was the time when the livestock was slaughtered and the final harvest was gathered before the inevitable plunge into the depths of winter's darkness. Fires were lit to help wandering spirits on their way, and offerings were given in the names of the gods and the ancestors. Seen as a beginning, Samhain is now often called the Witches' New Year. We honor our ancestors, wind down our activities, and get ready for the months of intro-spection ahead... and the cycle continues.

The Modern Pagan's Relationship to the Wheel

Modern Pagans take inspiration from many pre-Christian spiritual traditions, exemplified by the Wheel of the Year. The cycle of eight festivals we recognize throughout modern Pagandom today was never celebrated in full by any one particular pre-Christian culture. In the 1940s and 1950s, a British man named Gerald Gardner created the new religion of Wicca by drawing on a variety of cultures and traditions, deriving and adapting practices from pre-Christian religion, animistic beliefs, folk magick, and various shamanic disciplines and esoteric orders. He combined multicultural equinox and solstice traditions with Celtic feast days and early European agricultural and pastoral celebrations to create a single model that became the framework for the Wiccan ritual year.

This Wiccan ritual year is popularly followed by Wiccans and witches, as well as many eclectic Pagans of various stripes. Some Pagans only observe half of the sabbats, either the quarters or the cross-quarters. Other Pagans reject the Wheel of the Year altogether and follow a festival calendar based on the culture of whatever specific path they follow rather than a nature-based agrarian cycle. We all have such unique paths in Paganism that it is important not to make any assumptions about another's based on your own; maintaining an open and positive attitude is what makes the Pagan community thrive.

Many Pagans localize the Wheel of the Year to their own environment. Wicca has grown to become a truly global religion, but few of us live in a climate mirroring Wicca's British Isles origins. While traditionally Imbolc is the beginning of the thaw and the awakening of the earth, it is the height of winter in many northern climes. While Lammas may be a grateful celebration of the harvest for some, in areas prone to drought and forest fires it is a dangerous and uncertain time of year.

There are also the two hemispheres to consider. While it's winter in the Northern Hemisphere, it's summer in the Southern Hemisphere. While Pagans in America are celebrating Yule and the Winter Solstice, Pagans in Australia are celebrating Midsummer. The practitioner's own lived experiences are more important than any dogma written in a book when it comes to observing the sabbats.

In that spirit, you may wish to delay or move up celebrations so that the seasonal correspondences better fit your own locale, or you may emphasize different themes for each sabbat as you experience it. This series should make such options easily accessible to you.

No matter what kind of place you live on the globe, be it urban, rural, or suburban, you can adapt sabbat traditions and practices to suit your own life and environment. Nature is all around us; no matter how hard we humans try to insulate ourselves from nature's cycles, these recurring seasonal changes are inescapable. Instead of swimming against the tide, many modern Pagans embrace each season's unique energies, whether dark, light, or in between, and integrate these energies into aspects of our own everyday lives.

Llewellyn's Sabbat Essentials series offers all the information you need in order to do just that. Each book will resemble the one you hold in your hands. The first chapter, *Old Ways*, shares the history and lore that have been passed down, from mythology and pre-Christian traditions to any vestiges still seen in modern life. *New Ways* then spins those themes and elements into the manners in which modern Pagans observe and celebrate the sabbat. The next chapter focuses on *Spells and Divination* appropriate to the season or based in folklore, while the following one, *Recipes and Crafts*, offers ideas for decorating your home, hands-on crafts, and recipes that take advantage of seasonal offerings. The chapter *Prayers and Invocations* provides ready-made calls and prayers you may use in ritual, meditation, or journaling. The *Rituals of Celebration* chapter provides three complete rituals: one for a solitary, one for two people, and one for a whole group such as a coven, circle, or grove. (Feel free to adapt each or any ritual to your own needs, substituting your own offerings, calls, invocations, magickal workings, and so on.

When planning a group ritual, try to be conscious of any special needs participants may have. There are many wonderful books available that delve into the fine points of facilitating ritual if you don't have experience in this department.) Finally, in the back of the book you'll find a complete list of correspondences for the holiday, from magickal themes to deities to foods, colors, symbols, and more.

By the end of this book, you'll have the knowledge and the inspiration to celebrate the sabbat with gusto. By honoring the Wheel of the Year, we reaffirm our connection to nature so that as her endless cycles turn, we're able to go with the flow and enjoy the ride.

OLD WAYS

beginnings, birth, renewal, rejuvenation, balance, fertility, change
strength, vernal equinox, sun enters Aries, Libra in the You
Green Man, Amalthea, Aphrodite, Blodeuwedd, Eostre, Ea
Flora, Freya, Gaia, Guinevere, Persephone, Libera, Me
pet, Umaj, Vela, Aengus MacOg, Cernunnos, Herma, The
ama, Mabon Osiris, Pan, Thor, abundance, growth, health, ea
l healing, patience understanding virtue, spring, honor, contentme
hic abilities, spiritual truth, intuition, receptivity, love, inner se
rovement, spiritual awareness, purification, childhood, innocence,
ly, creativity, communication, concentration, divination, harmor
bilities, prosperity, attraction, blessings, happiness, luck, money,
, guidance, visions, insight, family, wishes, celebrating life cyc
endship, courage, attracts love, honesty, good health, emotions,
improvement, influence, motivation, peace, rebirth, self preserva
nine power, freedom, optimism, new beginnings, vernal equinox
creation, sun, apple blossom, columbine, crocus, daffodil, daisy,
sy, honeysuckle, jasmine, jonquil, lilac, narcissus, orange blossom,
rose, rose, the fool, the magician, the priestess, justice, the star
, gathering, growth, abundance, eggs, seeds, honey, dill, asparag

$\mathcal{T}$HE SUN SHINES brightly overhead as witches dance around a bonfire and feast on fruits and vegetables fresh from the fields. Children laugh and play, rolling wheels that symbolize the sun and chasing shining bubbles that float through the air like faeries. It is the Summer Solstice, also known as Midsummer or Litha. The earth rejoices in abundance and light, and so do we.

Midsummer is the longest day of the year and the shortest night. The sun has reached its zenith and is at the height of its power magickally as well. After today, the days will grow imperceptibly shorter, moving us into the dark half of the year. At the Winter Solstice, the entire process reverses, and we will move again toward the light of Midsummer.

In the Northern Hemisphere, the Summer Solstice falls around June 21, at the point when the sun enters Cancer (or Capricorn in December, if you are in the southern half of the world). It is a celebration of the sun, of fire, and of the bounty of the land.

Historically, Midsummer has been observed in virtually every culture in the world at one point or another. The Greeks,

Romans, Celts, Norse, Aztecs, and Jews all celebrated the longest day of the year in their own ways, with their own gods. But across all of these different cultures, certain themes are usually associated with this particular day.

For instance, since the sun is at its highest point, Midsummer is almost always celebrated as a solar festival, a fire festival, or both. Although in many places there was a water component as well, including pilgrimages to sacred wells or other bodies of water. Bonfires were common, and it was not unusual for vigils to be held from dawn on Midsummer Day until the sun came up the following morning.

Although not a harvest festival like the three sabbats that follow it, the Summer Solstice was still a celebration of nature, growing things in all their forms, and the crops now planted in the fields. The holiday often focused on fertility, abundance, prosperity, success, and good fortune to mirror the enthusiastic growth of the surrounding countryside.

In Celtic traditions, June was the month of the oak—an important and much-valued tree that was seen as the symbol of strength and vitality. In the modern Pagan mythos, the year is split between the old and wise Oak King, who rules from the Winter Solstice to the Summer Solstice, and the young, energetic Holly King, who is supreme from Midsummer to Yule.

It is believed that the Druids gathered sacred herbs on this day, and even today we often harvest plants on Midsummer for use in magick, healing, and food preparation. Many of our modern-day practices on this holiday can be traced back to roots in earlier Pagan rites and rituals.

Midsummer is one of the great fire festivals, as is fitting for a day when the sun burns hot overhead. In many cultures, it was customary to light bonfires, often on the tops of hills where they could be seen for miles. People did circle dances around the fire or rolled burning wheels down the hillside.

It was also considered to be the most auspicious day to commune with the Fae or faerie people, as it was supposed that contact was easier during the "between" times, when one season transitioned to another. The faerie folk are also drawn to sweet-smelling flowers, honey and nectar, and other elements most readily available at this time of year.

Shakespeare used this tradition as the basis of one of his most popular plays, *A Midsummer Night's Dream*, in which the mischievous faerie folk cause all sorts of havoc and confusion during a Midsummer celebration.

The full moon in June was also known as the Honey Moon, and many people married during this time. (It was sometimes believed to be bad luck to marry in May, when the god and goddess held their own sacred rites.) Undoubtedly this was part of what inspired Shakespeare to use so many weddings in his play, including the main reason for the dramatic celebration, the marriage of Theseus, the Duke of Athens, to Hippolyta, the Queen of the Amazons.

The Calendar and the Astrological Cycle

The Summer Solstice is one of two yearly solstices, the other being the Winter Solstice, at the opposite end of the year. Technically, the solstice itself falls at the exact moment that Earth's semi-axis is most inclined toward the sun, which occurs twice a year. So in the Northern Hemisphere, the Summer Solstice occurs in June, and the Winter Solstice occurs in December. In the Southern Hemisphere, the reverse is true.

The Summer Solstice tends to fall around June 21, although the date can vary from June 20 to June 22 in the Northern Hemisphere, and December 20 to December 23 in the Southern Hemisphere. Because the moment of the solstice changes with the longitude, each place on the planet only hits that "true" solstice for a minute, and the exact minute it is will change with your location.

Fortunately, few of us will ever have to track down that exact moment, since most people celebrate the entire day of Midsummer, some even beginning at Midsummer Eve the night before. The dates can be found on most modern calendars.

The word solstice comes from the Latin: *sol* for "sun," and *stitium* meaning "to stand still." To the ancient people, it may have seemed that the sun was in fact standing still in the sky, and they often prayed to various sun gods on this day. This includes some familiar names, including the Greek Apollo, the Egyptian Ra, and the Irish Lugh, as well as some lesser-known gods, such as Belinos, the Celtic sun god who causes the sacred herbs of Midsummer to grow.

Early Pagans lived on the land and depended on it to live. Most ancient holidays center around the growth and harvest cycle: whether it was the time to plant seeds, the time to tend the crops, the time to harvest, or the time to rest in the winter's darkness and wait for the cycle to begin again. Because their survival depended on a successful harvest, as well as plentiful wildlife and cooperative weather, these cultures often prayed to gods and goddesses who affected these things, and celebrated the days that marked the passage of the year.

The Summer Solstice was an especially joyful holiday because in most places it marked the end of the planting season and the beginning of the earliest harvest. The day was often seen as an excuse to take a moment out of the never-ending work of growing and finding food, and allow all those busy people to catch their breath for just a moment and enjoy the fruits of their labors before resuming their tasks the next day.

Midsummer is not actually in the middle of the summer for everyone in every climate, despite falling between the Spring Equinox (about March 21) and the Fall Equinox (about September 21). In upstate New York, for example, "real" spring starts somewhere from the middle to the end of April, with the occasional snowfall seen at the very beginning of May. So summer has barely begun when the middle of June rolls around. In Texas or southern California, the temperatures may already be scorching hot and dry.

The seasons vary greatly depending on which part of the country, and indeed the world, you reside in. Summer in California and Florida is very different from summer in New York, Canada, or Finland. But the basics are the same: there is still more light and warmth than at other times of the year, and the energy of the earth is abundant and accessible. By the time of the Summer Solstice, summer is definitely in the air. The warm-weather birds have returned, the days are warm, and all around nature is blossoming. There is little wonder that we—and our ancestors—celebrate the longest day of the year!

Ancient Sites

It is thought that an ancient culture built Stonehenge as a way of marking the arrival of the solstice, and NASA lists it as one of the five oldest observatories in the world. The gigantic stones were transported from Welsh mountains that were about 240 miles from Stonehenge's location in Wiltshire, England, on the Salisbury Plain, although how that was accomplished between 3100 and 1500 BCE has never been explained (Carr-Gomm, 115).

Many scholars believe that the site was used for important Druidic rites, although there has been no definitive proof of that theory. (Nor, in fact, was the henge built by the Druids, despite most assumptions to the contrary.) However, modern Druids and others still gather there by the thousands to greet the sun. Unlike many other sites, which were designed to highlight the sun either at dawn or as it set, at Stonehenge, there are three different alignments, at sunrise, noon, and sunset.

Other lesser-known solstice-oriented constructions can be found around the world. Not so far away, on Mount Seskin in the Tallaght Hills of Ireland, the sun's first rays on the solstice are reflected into a pool of water found amid a number of standing stone sites that are scattered across the mountain. The Exernsteine rock spires near Horn-Bad Meinberg, Germany, are natural formations that became a place of pilgrimage for various cultures. No one knows which one of them built the prehistoric temple that is found on the top of the highest spire, but inside this temple there is a hole above the altar that aligns to the sun during the Summer Solstice (Carr-Gomm, 108).

In the mysterious deserted ruins in places like Fajada Butte in the Chaco Canyon of New Mexico, there are signs that the earliest Native American peoples tracked the passage of the sun and created a hole in the south wall that directs the sunlight toward carvings known as petroglyphs. Other Native American sites have also been found with astrological features, including

Serpent Mound in Ohio, a 1,370-foot-long structure in the shape of a snake with its head facing the sunset on Midsummer (Carr-Gomm, 154; Pritchard).

In Egypt, the setting sun on the Summer Solstice hits a point exactly in the center between the two largest of the Great Pyramids. At the Osireion Temple at Abydos, believed for centuries to be the burial place of the god Osiris, the sun shines through a gap in the nearby Libyan hills and strikes the temple walls on the day of Midsummer.

Also in Egypt is the Essene Monastery, home to the mystical Jewish sect that wrote the Dead Sea Scrolls. The Essenes followed a solar calendar, rather than the traditional Jewish lunar calendar. The monastery was designed to highlight the setting sun on the Summer Solstice. At Nabta Playa, in the midst of the Egyptian desert, a set of stone megaliths bearing an amazing resemblance to Stonehenge have been shown to align not only with the Summer Solstice, but also a number of stars, including Sirius and Dubhe, the brightest stars in Orion's belt.

Buddhist monks in India are believed to be responsible for the Ajanta Caves, a series of thirty manmade caves carved out of the cliffs in a remote jungle. The caves all contained shrines to Buddha, and one of them contained a statue of the Buddha that was lit by the sun at dawn on the Summer Solstice.

It is clear from these examples, which are just the tip of the iceberg, that the Summer Solstice was observed across the world by numerous cultures in various ways. It was an important enough part of these cultures to merit permanent locations, many of which still remain standing to this day as an inspiration to us all.

General Historical Overview, Mythology & Lore

Midsummer celebrations took different forms in different cultures, although they often had certain elements in common. For instance, the sun and fire were often key elements, as were flowers, herbs, and growing things. Here are a few of the more prominent examples:

Ancient Greece

As befits a fire festival, the Summer Solstice was the time when the Titan Prometheus was said to have given the gift of fire to human beings, thus enabling them to go on and create civilized society. The goddess Athena was also considered to have solar attributes, and the Greek year began on the first new moon after the Summer Solstice. A holiday known as Panathenaia was held in her honor, and the people prayed to her to bring rain for the crops (Franklin, 8).

Ancient Romans

Midsummer was considered sacred to Juno, the Roman counterpart of Hera, who was married to Jupiter, the king of the gods. Like Hera, Juno was the goddess of marriage, which is one of the reasons June—the month named in her honor—has always been one of the most popular times to get married. Married women celebrated the goddess Vesta, who ruled over the hearth fires and the home, with the festival of Vestalia.

Ancient Chinese

The Chinese considered the Summer Solstice to be a Yin (female) holiday, and its counterpart, the Winter Solstice, to be Yang (male). Celebrations centered around fertility and the renewal of the earth, and the smoke from burned offerings was said to carry their prayers up into the heavens.

The Saxons, Norse, and Germanic Peoples

Midsummer was also mid-year for the Saxons, whose year began with the Winter Solstice. It is thought that the word *Litha*, often used as an alternative name for the Summer Solstice, may have originated with the Saxon name for the month of June, meaning "light" or "moon." (It actually entered popular use after J. R. R. Tolkien used the word *Litha* for a Midsummer festival in his Lord of the Rings trilogy.)

The Saxons celebrated Thor, the god of thunder, because he brought much-needed rains. The Germanic tribes originally celebrated the sun's triumphant ascension with huge bonfires.

After the Christians came, this holiday was adapted into the Feast of St. John (or *Johannisnacht,* which translates to "John's night"), which is often still observed by lighting fires on the hilltops. In Finland, the summer solstice was called *Juhannus*, and was an especially joyous occasion because of the light after many months of darkness. The Vikings met at Midsummer to deal with legal matters and resolve disputes. They built huge bonfires and made pilgrimages to sacred healing wells. Some of these traditions are still celebrated on Midsummer in Iceland.

The Celts and the Druids

Much of what we know about the ancient Celts and Druids is secondhand, since they didn't write things down. But it is believed that the Druids celebrated the Summer Solstice as representing the marriage of earth and heaven. They gathered sacred herbs, including mistletoe berries, to be used later for healing and magickal work. Their sacred tree, the oak, was burned in Midsummer fires, and they crowned an Oak King. The ancient Celts are thought to have used the light and energy of the sun to banish evil spirits and demons. They also lit bonfires and sent burning wheels down hills. Couples would jump through the flames for luck, and the higher they jumped, the higher the crops would grow.

Other Areas of Europe

In ancient Gaul (a region of Western Europe during the Iron Age and Roman era, which covered the territory that includes present-day France, Luxembourg, Belgium, most of Switzerland, and Northern Italy, as well as the parts of the Netherlands and Germany), the Midsummer celebration was called the Feast of Epona, in honor of the goddess of fertility, agriculture, and horses. In Russia, the Midsummer holiday was known as Kupalo, from the verb *kupati* (to bathe) and was celebrated by mass baths on Midsummer morning. In Portugal, it was believed that water possessed special healing powers on St. John's Eve. (*Spiritual Humanism*) A Midsummer tree and Maypole dances are still a focus of Swedish celebrations.

Native Americans

Midsummer celebrations were common among many Native American tribes. The Hopi Indians of Arizona held dances featuring kachinas (masked dancers), who represented the spirits of fertility and rain, and took messages to the gods. The Sioux and the Natchez perform ceremonial sun dances. Many of these traditions continue to the present day.

Gods & Goddesses

As the Wheel of the Year turns, the God and Goddess change their forms as well, altering with the seasons. The triple goddess, who can manifest as Maiden, Mother, or Crone, is in her Mother aspect at Midsummer, pregnant with the child of her consort, the God. In some traditions, the God is strong and virile; at the peak of his power, reflecting the glory and power of the sun up above. In others, he sacrifices himself so that the land might flourish and the crops grow. (In other traditions, this doesn't occur until the next sabbat, Lughnasadh, or occasionally, not until Mabon, the Autumn Equinox.)

In her classic book, *The Spiral Dance*, Starhawk puts it this way:

> *Now on this longest day, light triumphs, and yet begins the decline into the dark. The Sun King grown embraces the Queen of Summer in the love that is death because it is so complete that all dissolves into the single song of ecstasy that moves the worlds. So the Lord of Light dies to Himself, and sets sail across the dark seas of time, searching for the isle of light that is rebirth. (205)*

This might be interpreted to mean that on Midsummer itself, the God is alive, strong, and full of love for both his Goddess wife and his land. It is only after the sun sets on the Summer Solstice that he begins to die, just as the light slowly dies away.

Many ancient cultures reflected much of this sentiment in their own celebrations, despite the fact that their own belief structure may not have matched our modern ones. There were any number of gods and goddesses who were specifically honored at Midsummer, but many of them fall into a few specific categories: sun gods and goddesses, fire gods and goddesses, war and/or thunder gods, sometimes healer or water gods and goddesses, love goddesses, mother goddesses, and pregnant goddesses.

Here are some of the goddesses most commonly associated with and celebrated at Midsummer:

- Aestas, Roman goddess of summer—Midsummer is her sacred time.

- Aine, Celtic sun/fire goddess—Her Midsummer festival features a torch-lit procession and a vigil. Her name means "bright spark." She is also thought to be the queen of the faeries.

- Amaterasu, Japanese sun goddess—Central goddess of the Shinto religion, Amaterasu is known as the goddess "from whom all light comes."

- Anuket, Egyptian goddess of the Nile—The Nile traditionally flooded at the time of the Summer Solstice, bringing fertility to the land, so Anuket was worshipped as Nourisher of the Fields.

- Aphrodite, Greek goddess of love, especially sexual love—She was born from the waves.

- Benten (also Benzaiten), Japanese goddess of love—A festival in her name is still celebrated at Midsummer.

- Brigantia, Celtic goddess of summer (sometimes confused with Brigid)—She is the goddess of fire, healing, fertility, and sacred wells. At Midsummer she is said to spread the fire of creativity and inspiration.

- Iarila, Russian sun goddess whose name means "ardent sun"—Celebrated at the Summer Solstice with fire and water together with her brother/mate Iarilo. Figures of the siblings are burned in effigy at Midsummer; they were also known under the names Lada and Lado, Kupal'nitsa and Kupalo, and later were Christianized into Mary and Ivan (from which came St. Ivan's Day, a variation on St. John's Day).

- Saule/Saules mate, Baltic sun goddess—Her name means "sun." She is married to the moon.

- Solntse, Slavic sun goddess—She was married to her husband the moon on Midsummer.

And here are some of the gods:

- Agni, Hindu fire god—His lightning brings rain to fertilize the land.

- Apollo, Greek/Roman god of healing, music, and the sun—He drove his chariot across the sky each morning to bring the sun.

- Balder/Baldur, Scandinavian/Norse god of light—He was born at the Winter Solstice and dies at the Summer Solstice.

- Hoder/Hodur, Norse counterpart of Balder, god of the dark—He was born at the Summer Solstice and dies at the Winter Solstice.

- Janus, Roman god of doorways—He has two faces which look both forward and backward. Janus watches over the turn of the year.

- Kupalo, Slavic/Russian god of peace—He is celebrated at Midsummer with water rituals.

- Ra, Egyptian sun god—He created the world.

Alternative Names

Most Pagan holidays have more than one name. This can be a matter of general usage, such as Midsummer, or names that have come into more common use since the advent of modern Paganism and Witchcraft, such as Litha. And of course, different cultures have different names, even if they often translate to mean the same thing. There are also what can be called "associated holidays," which take place around the same time of the year, and which can be celebrated either in conjunction with the sabbat, or separately, if there is one that appeals to you (a festival for a particular goddess, for instance).

Here are some of the alternative names for Midsummer: Alban Heflin (Modern Druids), Enyovden (Bulgaria), Feast of the Sun (Aztec), Feill-Sheathain (Scottish), Gathering Day, Ivan Kupala Day (Russia), Juhannas (Germany), Litha (Modern Pagan, possibly Saxon), Méan Samhraidh (Celtic), Sonnenwende (Norse/German—Sun's Turning, used for both Summer and Winter Solstice), Summer Solstice, and Thing-Tide (Scandinavian).

Traditional Symbols for Midsummer

One way to make your Midsummer ritual or celebration more meaningful is to integrate some of the classic symbols for the holiday, many of which have been used in various cultures for centuries. (Summer has a lot of the same traits no matter where you are, after all.)

These can include actual symbols, of course, but also plants, animals, colors, and more. This is a basic list, with a few suggestions for how to incorporate these elements into your ritual, but you can always add anything else that seems right to you. As with all other magickal practice, there is no one "right" way to do things, and it is important to listen to your heart.

Animals

Bees: Symbols of abundance, messengers from the spirits, new life and good health, sweetness. Use honey in your ritual, or make honey cakes or mead for your feast, if you are having one. Put out a little honey in a dish for the faeries. Burn beeswax candles. Plant flowers that are particularly attractive to bees (like the aptly named bee balm, for instance). Take a moment during your ritual to thank the bees for their hard work pollinating plants so that the crops will grow.

Bull: Symbols of fertility, power, strength (associated with the god and kingship). Unlike the Pagans of ancient times, you are unlikely to roast an entire bull. But you can certainly throw a couple of steaks on the grill, if you happen to be a meat-eater. You can use symbols for the Zodiac sign Taurus, the bull, ♉, on your altar, or the rune symbol *Uruz*, which represents the wild ox, ᚢ, and therefore stands for strength of will, power, and health.

Butterflies: Symbol of rebirth (they change from an inert chrysalis to beautiful flying creature) and the soul. Put silk or paper butterflies on your altar, or hang them where they will flutter in the breeze (in an open window, maybe). Like the bees, butterflies sip nectar from flowers and spread pollen that then pollinates the plants, so you can thank them as well, and plant some of the flowers they like. The regal Monarch butterfly exists primarily on milkweed, which can be hard for them to find. Try planting some, or putting a symbolic milkweed pod on your altar. Since butterflies are a symbol for change, you may want to cut out a piece of paper in the shape of a butterfly, write on it the things you would like to change, and then burn it as a part of your ritual. Visualize yourself going into a cocoon and coming out as your best, most beautiful self.

Cow: Symbol of abundance, mother goddesses (because of the milk cows give), and wealth. To celebrate the cow, serve milk or cheese dishes at your feast, or make cheese bread for your cakes and ale (the portion of a ritual where food and/or drink are consumed both for celebration and for grounding). Place a couple of cow figurines on your altar, or a picture of Hathor, the cow-headed Egyptian goddess of the sky. You can also use the rune symbol *Fehu*, ᚠ, which stood for cattle in the original Norse usage and represents wealth (or good fortune you work hard for) and fulfillment.

Hawk and Eagles: Seen as solar birds because they soared so high, they are also symbols of power and strength. Hawks, eagles, and falcons have always been associated with the sun, probably because they fly so high, it seems as though they are flying up to the sun itself. Eagles were the symbol of the Egyptian sun god Ra, represented solar power to the Aztecs, were messengers for the Greek god Zeus, and generally used to symbolize the renewal of the spirit and the triumph of life over death. It is illegal in most parts of the country to collect or own eagle feathers, but you can use the feather of a lesser bird to represent the eagle, hawk, or falcon. Likewise, you can have a picture or a statue on your altar. If you are dancing around a bonfire, spread your arms out and pull the energy of these fierce birds into your own spirit as you send it into flight.

Horse: Symbol of power, strength, swiftness, and virility. Horses can symbolize the sun, the land, freedom, and energy. The image of a horse running untamed across an ancient plain evokes feelings of wildness and joy. In many myths, horses were used to pull the chariots of the sun across the sky, bringing the light in the morning and taking it away in the evening. You can invoke the goddess Epona, an ancient mother goddess who was often depicted riding a horse, or Apollo, whose sun chariot was drawn by four horses named Pyrios, Aeos, Aethon, and Phlegon. Use a horse statue, picture, or symbol if you need a boost of vitality or to tap into some of their speed and strength. A horseshoe can be used to represent the horse as well, and is useful if you are doing magickal work for luck and success.

Swallows, Wrens, and Other Summer Birds: These birds are associated with the return of the sun. Birds that migrate are often considered to be symbols of the season, since their return heralds the return of the sun. If you can be outside on Midsummer, take some time to listen to the bird songs and watch them fly overhead. Waft the incense or sage you use during ritual with a feather, or put out some birdseed to thank them for their presence. If you find an egg on the ground, you can put that on your altar (never take one from a nest, unless you are certain the nest is abandoned).

Symbols

Balefire or Bonfire: Other than the sun itself, the bonfire (also called a balefire or needfire) is probably the most universally used symbol of Midsummer, shared by almost every culture from the Aztecs to the Romans. Different lands had different traditions, but many of them included lighting a bonfire on a hilltop or near a sacred well, dancing around it or leaping over it, burning specific types of woods (often, but not always oak), and burning images, flowers, or herbs in the fires. Animals were sometimes driven through the dying embers for health and protection in the year to come, and chunks of burned wood leftover when the fires died out were saved for luck or later magickal workings. If you have a bonfire on Midsummer, be sure to keep a few pieces of the coals.

Circles and Disks: Circles and disks are simple representations of the sun. Many of the most ancient cultures have petroglyphs (drawings on rock or cave walls) featuring simple circles or disks to represent the sun. If you need to do something less than obvious, this is a good symbol to use.

Equal Arm Crosses and Swastikas: Swastikas (equal arm crosses with ends on the arms) were originally symbols used in Hindu and Scandinavian cultures, associated with good luck and movement through the cycle of the year. They are rarely used today because of their negative connotations. Equal arm crosses, however, also represent the four quarters of the year (the two solstices and two equinoxes), and are more acceptable. Celtic crosses and Brighid's crosses are two common examples. Simple equal arm crosses can be made from crossing two pieces of wood and tying them together with ribbon, yarn, or strips of willow. If you want to make one to throw into a bonfire, use oak or hazel, if you can find them. If you want, you can tuck a piece of paper with a spell or a prayer written on it into the binding.

Faeries: Faeries represent the magickal world. There are three times in the Wheel of the Year that are considered optimum for connecting with the faeries; Midsummer, May Eve (the night before Beltane), and Samhain. Faeries are rarely seen, but their presence can sometimes be felt, or they will leave behind signs of their passage, since they are often mischievous and fond of playing tricks on unsuspecting humans. If you wish to stay in their good graces, it is best to leave them small gifts or offering, such as fragrant flowers or a tiny bowl of honey or mead. Always be polite and respectful when dealing with them; although modern images show them as being tiny and cute, ancient stories do not always agree, and it is best to be cautious.

Herbs: Everything that grows is celebrated on Midsummer, but traditionally it is also considered the most auspicious time to gather any herbs you want to use for healing or magickal work in the year to come. Of course, not everything is ready to be harvested yet, but if you have an herb garden, this is a good day to gather whatever herbs have reached maturity. You can use a boline—the white-handled knife many witches reserve for cutting plants—or any other clean tool. Harvest at dawn, when the dew is still on the plants, or at noon, when the sun is high. Magickal plants, such as vervain, yarrow, and St. John's Wort are particularly good herbs to harvest on Midsummer. If you want, you can then use some of the newly cut plants in your Midsummer ritual.

Rose: A beautiful flower often associated with love goddesses such as Venus and Aphrodite, the rose is usually in bloom at this time of the year and can be used to decorate your altar. Rose petals or rose hips (the fruit of the rose bush) can also be used in ritual, especially any involving love magick.

Sacred Wells: All across Europe, and in some other countries as well, people made pilgrimages to sacred wells on Midsummer for healing and blessings. Often, these wells were only visited on a solstice or other special days. While most of these sites are gone now, a few remain, and if you live near or are visiting an area where there is one, it might be worth the trip on Midsummer. These wells were sometimes considered to be places of transition, between our world and another, or symbolic of the womb of the earth and/or a mother goddess.

The Sun Wheel: The wheel was often used as a symbol of the sun's journey across the sky, or the chariot that pulled it. Burning wheels were often rolled down hills on Midsummer. (I don't particularly recommend trying this at home …)

Spinning/Spinning Wheels: Many of the goddesses associated with Midsummer were also associated with the craft of spinning or weaving.

Spirals: Another very ancient symbol dating back to the beginning of time, it is thought to have represented the sun's travels, as well as the journey from life to death and back again.

The Sun: The most common representation of Midsummer is the sun itself. Whether it was the actual sun overhead, flowers that resembled the sun, or any of the symbols such as fire, wheels, or disks that were used to stand for the sun, almost all Midsummer celebrations are focused on the sun's position high in the sky, as well as its power and energy.

Not all of these symbols translate equally well to the modern world, but you can choose the traditions and associations that resonate with you and your life and integrate them into your personal Midsummer practice.

NEW WAYS

...ception, ...ness, ...ation, ...ness, jealousy, change,
strength, vernal equinox, sun enters Aries, Libra in the Tou...
Green Man, Amalthea, Aphrodite, Blodeuwedd, Eostre, Eo...
, Flora, Freya, Gaia, Guinevere, Persephone, Libera, As...
...pet, Umaj, Vila, Aengus MacOg, Cernunnos, Herma, The
...ama, Mabon Osiris, Pan, Thor, abundance, growth, health, ca...
l healing, patience understanding virtue, spring, honor, contentm...
...hic abilities, spiritual truth, intuition, receptivity, love, inner se...
...rovement, spiritual awareness, purification, childhood, innocence
...ty, creativity, communication, concentration, divination, harmo...
...bilities, prosperity, attraction, blessings, happiness, luck, money
..., guidance, visions, insight, family, wishes, celebrating life cyc...
...endship, courage, attracts love, honesty, good health, emotions,
...improvement, influence, motivation, peace, rebirth, self preserva...
...mune power, freedom, optimism, new beginnings, vernal equinox
...creation, sun, apple blossom, columbine, crocus, daffodil, daisy
...sy, honeysuckle, jasmine, jonquil, lilac, narcissus, orange blossom
...rose, rose, the fool, the magician, the priestess, justice, the star,
..., gathering, growth, abundance, eggs, seeds, honey, dill, aspara...

$\mathcal{E}$ACH TIME OF year has its own particular energy, and the sabbats reflect that energy. For instance, at Imbolc, the energy is quiet and preparatory—waiting for the land to reawaken. At the Spring Equinox, the energy is bubbly and hopeful as new life springs forth. Midsummer energy is just that—energetic. The sun is energy, after all, and the earth is bursting with growth and vitality.

This seasonal energy dictates the general themes of the holiday as well as the kinds of magickal work usually done on or around that day. At Midsummer, the primary themes are abundance, growth, fertility, and increase of every kind. This means that the Summer Solstice is a good time for working on prosperity or anything positive that you want to continue to grow.

The mother goddesses and pregnant goddesses are honored, which can mean a ritual celebrating the goddess in her Mother aspect, or actual celebrations of mothers, family, and/or pregnancy.

This sabbat is a good time to connect with the earth, growing things in general, and the faerie folk (with all due respect and caution, of course). Green magick of every kind is practiced on this day. Traditionally, it has also been connected with healing, especially in conjunction with sacred wells and other bodies of water.

Love is often a focus, whether it is the love of mother for child, our love for our Mother the earth and our Father the sun, or romantic love. Love goddesses are often called upon for their blessings and assistance, and weddings and handfastings may take place as part of the Summer Solstice celebration.

Of course, the major theme of Midsummer has always been a celebration of the sun. This can manifest as a fire or sun ritual, honoring the God at his peak, bidding farewell to the light half of the year, or simply reveling in the light and energy of the season.

Empowerment, increase, abundance, love, and joy are the themes of Midsummer, and they have been through the centuries in many cultures around the world. It is the longest day of the year, and the sun fills the sky with light and energy. Our ancestors used the Summer Solstice to celebrate these things, and so do we.

Ancient Energies in a Modern World

Most of the Pagan holidays that have been passed on to us are based on an agricultural calendar. They honored a lifestyle lived without electricity or indoor plumbing, at the mercy of the weather, and completely dependent on whatever food could be raised or hunted locally.

Very few modern witches and Pagans have lives that remotely resemble those of our ancestors. (For which most of us are sincerely grateful. Did I mention indoor plumbing?) We have artificial lighting and don't need to confine the majority of our activities to the hours when the sun is in the sky. This means we tend to lose track of much of the seasonal restrictions that so influenced earlier Pagans. Does it matter that the sun rises or sets earlier, or that the days are shorter, if all we have to do is turn on a lamp to extend the day?

We also get all or most of our food from a grocery store, some of it coming from countries far away. Our meat is prepackaged and wrapped in plastic, distancing our connection to the animals it came from. We are no longer limited to eating only those items that are in season or that grow in the area of the country where we live. A drought or an early freeze might drive up the prices of that food, but most of us will never be at risk of starving because bad weather ruined our crops. (Although those who garden extensively will certainly curse the loss of time and effort we've put into the endeavor.)

Considering that most of the holidays we celebrate were based on conditions very different from the ones we live in, are they even still relevant? How do we continue to make a connection between our world and the world of our ancestors while also making sure that we are creating a holiday that applies to our own, modern reality? Thankfully, it is not as difficult as it might seem.

The sabbats, after all, are based not just on changing circumstances and environments, but also on the energies of the earth below, the seasonal cycle, and the sun overhead. These things have stayed more or less the same over the centuries, and still apply to us as they did to much earlier cultures. We just have to find ways to make that connection meaningful within the context of our own lives and our own personal approaches to a spiritual practice.

Midsummer and the Wheel of the Year

It is easy to ignore the ebb and flow of the seasonal energy when we are immersed in an artificial world. And frankly, most people don't have the option to retreat inside during the winter, huddling by the warmth of the fire and telling stories, getting up later and going to bed early because of the shorter days. Trying to do so would probably just get you fired!

But that doesn't mean we shouldn't pay attention to the shifts and changes of the natural energies altogether; they affect us in ways we are barely aware of. Trying to fight the natural flow of things can lead to stress, depression, and frustration, causing physical and psychological issues that reduce the enjoyment of our lives.

The Wheel of the Year gives us one way to tune in to those natural cycles, helping us to remember that our environment *is* artificial, and a different reality surrounds us, if we just take the time to connect with it. The sabbats are not only times for celebration, as they were for our ancestors, but also an opportunity to reestablish our relationship to the innate rhythms of the universe.

If you follow the Wheel as it turns, you will see that the energy of the planet moves through a predictable cycle of slow, quiet restfulness in the darker, colder months, through a rising awakening as the warmth and light increase and new life returns, into an exuberant burst of growth and abundance, before slowing back down again as the harvest is upon us and things begin to settle down, shut down, or die off as the darkness and cold return. And then the Wheel turns once more, and it all begins again.

When each of these parts of the cycle occurs, and how dramatic the changes are, depends on where you live. In some places, there are four drastically different seasons—when it is cold it is *cold*, when it is dark it is *dark*, and the shifting moods of nature are fairly difficult to ignore. In other places, the seasonal changes are moderate, and while the light still changes, the temperatures may not fluctuate all that much, and cold might mean sixty degrees Fahrenheit, instead of seventy-five. Nonetheless, the Wheel of the Year applies to everyone, in one way or another.

Midsummer falls midway between the Spring Equinox and the Fall Equinox, when the power of the cycle is at its peak. There is more light than there will be at any other time along the Wheel, and the energy will never be higher. This is the time for activity and forward movement. Unlike Imbolc, when we planned out the things we wished to work on during the course of the year—whether practical or spiritual—or Ostara (the Spring Equinox), when we planted the seeds for those things to come to pass, now is the time to be *doing* instead of thinking.

If you've been mulling over goals or laying the groundwork for future possibilities, Midsummer is your signal to *go, go, go*. Set out your plan of action and get it into motion. Use the power of the energy around you to help you be more motivated so you can achieve the things you set out to do. It's okay to stay up a little later, or get up a little earlier, as long as that feels right to you.

Midsummer is a good time to check in on your level of physicality, too. If you're like most people, you may spend much of your day inside, behind a desk—sitting. As the sun rises on Midsummer, it reminds us to get up and move—take a walk, go for a swim if you are lucky enough to have a body of water nearby, throw a stick for the dog, or simply dance around a bonfire. And keep moving, even after this day is over, as long as the light is strong in the sky. (It is best to keep active all year round, but the energy of the summer sun makes it easier for many of us.)

Use the light of the season to help you tune in to the internal light we all carry inside ourselves. Let the glow of the sun overhead remind you to look on the bright side, and to let your own inner light shine out for the rest of the world to see.

Midsummer is in some ways the most powerful holiday on the Wheel (although it could be argued that Samhain has some pretty amazing energy of a different type). Whether you use this power to move yourself forward, or simply channel it into a joyful celebration, it is clear why so many cultures observed this day in one form or another.

Country, City, or In-Between

How you honor these themes in your life and celebrate Midsummer will vary depending on where you live and what path you follow. Not everyone lives in the country with a large garden full of magickal herbs and a forest at their back door. It is a source of frustration for some Pagan and witchy folks when all the instructions for observing a holiday seem to start with "light a bonfire" or "dig a hole in the ground." It can be tough for city witches to stay in touch with nature, but on the other hand, they often have access to covens or open group festivals, which may not be true of those who live in more isolated rural areas. Folks who live in the suburbs may have space for a garden, but their yards are often out in full view of their neighbors, which can make dancing around in their magickal garb a little tricky, unless they are completely out of the broom closet. (Or simply don't care what the neighbors think.)

But not to worry—you can still enjoy your favorite Midsummer traditions, no matter where you live. It is all about being flexible and working with what you have available to you.

You can always find some way to celebrate Midsummer. If all else fails, you can work with the energies of love. After all, love is not limited by where you live, or whether or not you have a garden or can light a bonfire; it is universal, and available to us all. Call on goddesses of love, such as Aphrodite or Venus, or do a ritual focusing on your love for a significant other, your children, your pets, or even yourself. Send love out into the universe, and remember to open yourself up to receiving it back. It is Midsummer, and love is in the air, just like the rays of the sun high overhead.

Different Paths, Different Approaches

Although many Pagans and witches share common beliefs, we don't all celebrate the holidays in the same way. Midsummer celebrations tend to vary less than some of the other sabbats because the themes tend to be quite basic and universal. Nonetheless, there may be variations in approaches, and you will have to decide which one appeals most to you and works the best with your own practice.

For instance, Druids or Neodruids may try to celebrate Midsummer in ways that reproduce those hypothetically based on earlier Druid practices. They may wear white robes, use stone circles or wooded groves, and say invocations of Celtic gods and goddesses.

These same deities would be worshipped by Celtic (or Celtic Reconstructionist) Pagans, who would probably also focus on such traditional elements as bonfires, dancing, singing, divination, and other traditional Celtic practices.

Heathens, modern Pagans whose worship practice is taken from the pre-Christian traditions of Germany, Scandinavia, and Northern Europe, would be more likely to call on Germanic gods such as Balder. They also celebrate with bonfires, singing, and dancing. In the Heathen tradition, Midsummer is the second most important holiday of the year after Yule. Particularly Heathen additions to Midsummer rituals might include the making of wreaths and building small model Viking ships that will be used as burned offerings. They might refer to Midsummer by the name *Midsumarblot*.

Traditional Witchcraft is the name sometimes given to the form of Witchcraft practiced by those who do not label themselves as Wiccans or Neopagans. While this can cover a wide range of styles and approaches, those who consider themselves to be Traditional Witches usually follow a polytheistic or goddess-centered path based on traditional folk magick. The cultural background of the practitioner may be a major influence on exactly the type of magick that is practiced. Many Traditional Witches observe either the solstices and equinoxes or the quarter-cross holidays (such as Imbolc and Samhain), but not both. They tend to be solitary, so that any Midsummer celebration is likely to be a matter of magickal work, communing with nature, and whatever other traditions have been handed down.

Wiccans are a more modern type of Witchcraft/Pagan practice, based on earlier traditions but added to in numerous different ways. Wiccans can also vary greatly in their practices, but in general, they follow the Wheel of the Year and worship the Goddess in her changing forms as Maiden/Mother/Crone and a Horned God of some sort. Wiccans may be solitary or belong to covens, but many like to gather together for major sabbats such as Midsummer. A Wiccan Midsummer celebration might include honoring the goddess in her aspect as Mother, bonfires, drumming, and chanting. Divination, offerings for the faeries, and handfastings might also occur, as well as general salutations to the sun and an appreciation for summer's glories.

Many modern Pagans consider themselves to be Eclectic Witches, a form of Neopaganism that draws on the traditions and practices of many different cultures and paths. Eclectic Witches, who may or may not consider themselves to be Wiccans, tend to follow a nature-based path that focuses on the Wheel of the Year and the accompanying natural energies, worship some form of god and goddess (often numerous), and may practice on their own or in groups. As their name suggests, there is no one kind of Eclectic Witch, so their practices can vary widely. However, their Midsummer celebrations are likely to resemble those of Wiccans or Traditional Witches.

There is no right or wrong way to celebrate the Summer Solstice. Pagans base their celebrations on a combination of cultural traditions, historical practices, and their own personal inclinations.

Yearly Summer Solstice Festivals

While we no longer live in an era where Midsummer is celebrated in every village and town, if you really want to go to a major festival in honor of the Summer Solstice, there are a few places around the world that people flock to every year to do just that. You might want to consider looking to see if one of these is located anywhere near you, or you could combine your regular vacation plans with a chance to be someplace truly magickal on the longest day of the year.

The most well-known festival is probably held at Stonehenge, on the Salisbury Plain, located about eighty miles from London. More than 20,000 people have been known to gather at the mysterious standing stones that many associate with the Druids. If you want to visit Stonehenge, this is the day to do it; it is the only time that the public is allowed inside the circle of stones. Druids (or Neodruids, as the modern religion is sometimes referred to), also observe Midsummer at Glastonbury, England, as well as other lesser-known locations.

Across the country in Cornwall, the people of Penzance have revived the ancient *Golowan* ("Midsummer" in the Cornish language) celebration. The festival consists of Mazey Day and Quay Fair Day, and it includes musicians, artists, market stalls, and a large fireworks display. The town is adorned with greenery, much as it would have been in days gone by.

Elsewhere in Europe, the Summer Solstice is celebrated in a variety of ways. In Austria, a processional of ships sail down the Danube River past hilltop bonfires, fireworks, and glowing castle ruins. In Poland, a festival known as *Wianki* (wreaths) takes place in Krakow. There are live performances, prizes for the most beautiful wreath, and fireworks, among other entertainments.

In Bergen, Norway, the bonfire is something special. Known as the world's largest keg fire, it is created using kegs piled together by young people from a local music corps, which are then burned in celebration of the Norwegian Midsummer known as Sankthansaften.

Externsteine, Germany, is home to a natural outcropping of five limestone pillars that have been altered over time by man. Considered a sacred site both in ancient times and now, it draws numerous modern Pagans to its Summer Solstice celebrations.

In the United States, there are also a number of yearly festivals to celebrate Midsummer. In Santa Barbara, California, they hold a three-day party in honor of the holiday, including a parade, musicians and other entertainers, and much more. In Portland, Oregon, the large Lithuanian community uses the Solstice as an opportunity to get back to their roots, with a festival where people sing and dance until the sun sets. People make wreaths (flowers for the women and oak leaves for the men), jump over bonfires, and wash their faces in the morning dew as they greet the rising sun.

For something completely different, you can join in at the Solstice in Times Square celebration, where every year more than 8,000 people gather to practice yoga all day. This event started in 2002, and it has been steadily growing in popularity since then.

There are a few other celebrations that fall around the same time of year as the solstice, although they aren't actually linked to the holiday. For instance, there is the Fête de la Musique, which is held every year on June 21. It began in France, but now occurs in more than one hundred countries in Europe and across the world, and features all kinds of music.

How to Celebrate—Some Basic Suggestions

Obviously, how you choose to celebrate Midsummer will be based on which path you follow, your personal circumstances (whether you live in the city or the country, practice as a solitary or in a group, are in or out of the broom closet), as well as your needs or inclinations in any given year. It may even depend on whether or not it is raining that day.

If you are trying to decide what to do, however, here are a few basic suggestions for ways to observe the Summer Solstice. You can integrate as many or as few of these elements as you like into your own Midsummer ritual.

The Sun

Since Midsummer is traditionally focused on the sun, you can hold your ritual at noon, include representations of the sun (including the color yellow, sun disks or wheels, flowers that are associated with the sun, etc.), and offer up your appreciation to the sun god/goddess of your choice. You might also want to hold your ritual at dawn and greet the rising sun.

Obviously, on a day that celebrates the sun, it is good to find a way to go outside! (If it is raining, you may want to focus your attention on the rain/thunder gods associated with the holiday, rather than the sun god.) But if you can't have your ritual out under the open sky, there are other ways to keep the sun front and center. Try getting up with the first light of dawn on Midsummer Day and greeting the sun as it rises. You can also bid it farewell when it sets, too. If you have to have an indoor ritual, try to find a sunny space to do it in. Most Midsummer rituals are held either at noon or at dawn, but if the best sun of the day falls in the middle of your altar at two in the afternoon, you may want to observe the holiday then, just so you can stand in the light.

Fire

Bonfires are traditional at Midsummer, and you can have one that is as large or as small as you want. If you can't have an actual fire, candles or fire images will work as well. You can place candles around the outside boundary of your circle or use a fire pit to burn offerings. If you have a bonfire, you can throw in offerings of herbs, prayers written on pieces of paper, or simply dance around it in celebration.

Since Midsummer is a fire festival, it is nice to have a bonfire if you can. But if you don't have a good place to dig a fire pit, there are a number of other options. If you live in the city, check to see if there are any public rituals going on (or even non-Pagan solstice festivals, some of which happen every year); sometimes these folks can get permits or find places where a bonfire would be allowed. Bonfires, although traditional, aren't the only form of fire, either. If you have a barbecue grill that uses charcoal, that will work. If you have limited space, but have a balcony or outside spot, you can use a small, cast iron hibachi. Those who live near public parks may be able to find one that provides fire pits for campers or barbecue grills for picnickers. [Note: keep in mind that if you live in a part of the country that is at risk for forest fires at this time of the year, you may want to skip the outdoor fires during dry years, and be extra careful the rest of the time.]

If you can't make a large fire, try substituting candles. A cauldron or a fire-safe bowl can be filled with either sand or salt with a circle of small candles placed inside. If you can use beeswax candles, that's even better, since bees are one of the sacred creatures on Midsummer. For those who can't have an open flame at all (in a dorm room, for instance), you can purchase small cauldrons with fake flames made of ribbon; a battery-powered fan makes the ribbons move as if they were alive. There are also battery-powered LED tea lights that look almost like the real thing.

Water

Pilgrimages to sacred wells or other bodies of water played a part in many early rituals. Since the sacred water was usually associated with healing, try taking a bath with healing herbs before starting your formal ritual, or pass a bowl of water around your circle if you are celebrating with others. If you are fortunate enough to live near the ocean, a river, a stream, a lake, or a pond, you may want to make a pilgrimage of your own to thank the water for its gifts. Don't forget to bring a small offering for the guardians of the water.

For those who can't get to a natural source of water, you can still invoke the spirit of water in your own home. Try using a tabletop fountain or a bowl full of rainwater you collected ahead of time. Don't worry if you are limited to the water that comes out of your tap—after all, all water is connected, and at one point in time the water in your pipes may have been a drop in the ocean or the dew on a morning leaf. Bless and consecrate a bowl of water on your altar, and maybe leave it out in the light of the full moon preceding the holiday for some extra oomph. If it is a hot day, you can even try running through the sprinkler, if you have one.

Faeries

Midsummer is considered a powerful day to commune with the faery folk. Many traditions use this day to make offerings or gestures of good will to the Fae. If you will be celebrating outside, you can integrate an element of this into your ritual. Try placing flowers known to attract the faeries around the outside of your circle, or put out a bowl of milk. Do a ritual that includes asking for the blessings of the faeries. It is true that you are probably more likely to find faerie folk in the country; they're said to be uncomfortable around too much metal, especially cold iron, and are drawn to flowers, birds, and bees. But who can say that there aren't faeries in the city, too? Try putting out a bird feeder or placing a few colorful flowers in an open window. It may help to place a few small offering bowls out where they can find them: faeries like mead, it is said, and honey (which mead is made from), as well as small sweet treats. Some tales say they like milk, too. Pretty sparkly things may attract their attention. Remember when dealing with the Fae to always be respectful and polite. They can be quite tricky if annoyed.

Vigils

Numerous cultures hold vigils on Midsummer, either from dawn to dawn (Midsummer morning until the morning after) or sundown on Midsummer Eve to sundown on Midsummer Day. Try getting up with the sun on Midsummer Day and offering a formal greeting to it and to the sun god and/ or goddess of your choice. If you can, stay in a spiritual focus through the day, and then give a formal thanks to the sun either at sundown or at dawn the next morning. A vigil can be a powerful spiritual experience.

Handfastings

Midsummer is a traditional day for weddings and handfastings. If you are planning on having a Pagan wedding, you might want to hold it on Midsummer. (If you are including non-Pagans, you can explain the traditions to them.) A handfasting can be the ritual itself or part of a greater ritual. You may want to include elements of Midsummer traditions, such as holding your handfasting at noon to be out under the sun or having a bonfire either during or after the ritual. The chalice can hold sacred water to represent the holy wells that pilgrims might have gone to, or it can hold mead, which you can also share with the faeries. If you have a cute flower girl taking part, you might even want to dress her as a faery, and have her scatter rose petals around the outside of the ritual space as an enchanting way to cast the circle.

Light Half/Dark Half of the Year

In many cultures, Midsummer marks the point where the light half of the year gives way to the dark half of the year. Stage a mock battle between the Holly King and the Oak King, or give formal thanks to the light before acknowledging the coming darkness. If you are celebrating as a group, you can crown someone king for the next half of the year.

Celebrate Growth and Abundance

The natural world is in full blossom at Midsummer. Decorate your home or ritual circle with flowers, oak leaves, and/or harvest from your garden or local growers. Have a feast featuring food that is readily available at this time of year, with fresh fruit and vegetables, freshly baked bread, and traditional drinks such as mead or fruit juice. Do rituals that focus on abundance, growth, prosperity, and appreciation for nature.

In a perfect world, we would all be able to spend Midsummer in the middle of a meadow full of beautiful flowers, wandering through a garden, or looking over a countryside where greenery was bursting out all around us. But if you can't manage that, there are still plenty of ways to capture the feeling of the natural world's abundance and energy. Have a picnic in a park or your backyard with fruits and vegetables of the season (preferably grown as locally as possible). If you don't have a garden, buy some beautiful flowers and put them on your altar or in the middle of a table. Go for a walk and admire everything that is at its peak. Find an oak and pick up a few fallen leaves to take home with you. You can even hug it and pull some of its wonderful earthy strength deep inside. If you live in the city, you can try planting some flowers or herbs in a window box or tabletop container, timing a few of them to blossom or come to fruition as close to the day of the Summer Solstice as possible. And you can have a feast, no matter where you live.

Dance and Sing

Many early celebrations of Midsummer included circle dancing, singing, and general revelry. Try to include these elements in whatever ritual you do, whether it is solitary or with a group. Go online to find some chants you like and integrate them into your rites. Dancing, especially in a group around a bonfire, is a traditional part of many Midsummer celebrations. But you don't have to go to a large public festival in order to bring the magickal energy of dance into your ritual. If you have a bonfire, you can dance around it all by yourself. You can even dance around a candle in the middle of your living room. Or just put on a CD of some cool drumming or chanting that seems to you to capture the feeling of Midsummer, and dance wherever you are. It is more about the joyful movement than anything else, so don't worry about how you look—or "getting it right"—just dance.

Divination

You can include some form of divination in your celebration, using rune stones, tarot cards, or one of the many types of divination used traditionally in the various cultures. Divination to discover your true love was probably most practiced at this time.

Magick

Some traditions hold that Midsummer should only be used for celebration, while others believe it is one of the most powerful days of the year for magickal work. If you wish to practice some form of magick, Midsummer energies are perfect for prosperity, healing, love, power, creativity, fertility, and joy.

Harvest Herbs

Midsummer was often considered the best time to harvest herbs that would be used for magick and/or healing. If you have an herb garden, try mindfully harvesting some plants as part of your celebration of the holiday. As you clip them, focus on the sun's energy and power that are stored within their leaves and your intentions for their use later on. Give thanks to the elements that helped them grow. You may particularly want to harvest herbs and flowers associated with the Summer Solstice, such as yarrow, lavender, and St. John's Wort. Herbal charms and divinations will be covered in the next chapter, along with other varieties of spells and magickal work, a common way for Pagans to mark nearly any sabbat.

SPELLS
AND
DIVINATION

beginnings, birth, renewal, rejuvenation, balance, fertility, change

strength, vernal equinox, sun enters Aries, Libra in the Sou

Green Man, Amalthea, Aphrodite, Blodeuwedd, Eostre, Eo

Flora, Freya, Gaia, Guinevere, Persephone, Libera, M

pet, Umay, Vila, Aengus MacÓg, Cernunnos, Herma, The

ema, Mabon Osiris, Pan, Thor, abundance, growth, health, ca

healing, patience understanding virtue, spring, honor, contentm

tic abilities, spiritual truth, intuition, receptivity, love, inner se

movement, spiritual awareness, purification, childhood, innocence

ty, creativity, communication, concentration, divination, harmo

bilities, prosperity, attraction, blessings, happiness, luck, money

, guidance, visions, insight, family, wishes, celebrating life cyc

endship, courage, attracts love, honesty, good health, emotions,

improvement, influence, motivation, peace, rebirth, self preserva

unine power, freedom, optimism, new beginnings, vernal equinox

reation, sun, apple blossom, columbine, crocus, daffodil, daisy,

y, honeysuckle, jasmine, jonquil, lilac, narcissus, orange blossom,

rose, rose, the fool, the magician, the priestess, justice, the star

gathering, growth, abundance, eggs, seeds, honey, dill, aspara

*S*PELLS AND DIVINATION have always been part of the core tools of Witchcraft. Spells are a way of sending our intentions or requests out into the universe, and divination can be used to take in information from sources outside ourselves.

Both spells and divination require similar things: focus, intention, and belief. While you don't have to cast a formal magickal circle for either, it can sometimes be beneficial if you are doing serious work. Otherwise, you will simply need a quiet place and a space of time when you will be undisturbed. This is necessary to create the amount of focus you need to successfully cast a spell or work some form of divination.

Spellcasting can sometimes be aided by the use of tools that help us to increase our focus, such as candles, incense, music, crystals and gemstones, or the like. If you are going to be doing spells or divination work at Midsummer, you might find some of the basic correspondences at the back of the book helpful. You can also use the gods and goddesses, herbs and flowers, animals, and general symbols that were discussed in the previous chapter.

Litha is a perfect time for doing spellwork, especially anything that has to do with prosperity, abundance, healing, growth and change, and love. It is one of the best days of the year to work to increase power, strength, and energy and to simply celebrate your life with joy.

Divination is also traditionally done at the Summer Solstice, often at the transition times of dawn or dusk. You can use one of the ancient forms of divination or add your own modern touch. Just remember, whether you are casting a spell or casting the runes, focus your energy and will on whatever intention you are working with (such as the intention to bring in healing or to find answers to a pressing question) and to have faith that the universe will send you exactly what you need.

Midsummer, more than any other time of the year, is also perfect for doing spells for no other purpose than to celebrate the bounty and glory of nature, the joys of family and friends, and the light of the summer sun up above. On this day, these are more than enough.

A Set of Elemental Spells: Earth, Air, Fire, and Water

Healing Water Magick (Water Spell)

You don't need to have a sacred well in your neighborhood to be able to work healing water magick on the Summer Solstice.

This simple spell will channel those same energies, without the pilgrimage.

You will need a deep cauldron or bowl and enough water (if possible, use rain water or water from a river, a lake, or a spring) to fill the container almost to the top. You will also need a small bowl containing sea salt or regular salt, as well as the healing herbs of your choice (good options include elder flowers, lavender, lemon balm, yarrow, or vervain—you can use one, or a few, and other healing herbs may be substituted if you don't have these). Finally, bring a white or a yellow cloth. For an extra boost of power, you can put one of the Midsummer gemstones in the bottom of the bowl.

If possible, set the container full of water where the sun can hit it. If you can be outside, that's best, but if you have to be inside, try to find a spot where the sun will shine on the water. If the day is cloudy, or you don't have a suitable spot, visualize the sun instead.

Sit or kneel in front of the bowl of water with the salt, herbs, and cloth where you can reach them easily. See the rays of the sun dancing on the surface of the water, lending their power and energy to the water within. Take a deep breath, and say:

This water is pure and sacred.

Take a few grains of salt and sprinkle them on the water, saying:

Like the waves of the ocean and the tears of the Mother goddess,
the salt and the water are one, and sacred.

Crumble a small amount of the herbs in your hand and sprinkle them into the water, saying:

These healing herbs, the gift of the blossoming earth,
lend their healing powers to the water, and so too they are one,
and sacred.

Place your hands on either side of the cauldron or bowl and feel the energy of the water inside it. Close your eyes and see an ancient well, holy and powerful, then see that well transformed into the bowl between your hands. Open your eyes and dip your hands into the water. Leave them there for as long as you want, feeling the healing energy of the salt, herbs, and water traveling up your fingers and into your body. When you are done, hold your dripping hands up over the bowl and say:

This water is sacred and blessed, and so am I.

Dry your hands on the cloth. Either place the water on your altar for the rest of the day or pour it out after thanking it for its service.

Greet the Dawn (Air Spell)

It was traditional to greet the rising sun on the morning of the Summer Solstice. If possible, do this simple spell outside or in front of an open window facing east. If you don't have an east-facing window, you can use a different window or an altar placed toward the east.

You will need incense. Rose, lavender, pine, cinnamon, lemon, or orange are nice, but you can use whatever you prefer. You can also substitute a sage wand instead if you don't like incense.

Get out of bed in time to see the sun as it comes up. If you can, stand in front of an open window—or go outside—and actually watch the sunrise. As the sky begins to get brighter, light your incense, blow it gently into the air, and say:

> *Blessed sun, I greet your rays*
> *upon this sacred solstice day.*
> *Welcome be your warmth and light,*
> *bringing day out of the night.*
> *I greet the dawn with joyous heart,*
> *and so Midsummer now does start!*

Stand for a few moments with the sun on your face, sending the smoke of your incense out as an offering to the goddess of the dawn. Take in the energy of Midsummer and be filled with joy.

Fire Power Candle Magick (Fire Spell)

Fire is one of the major themes of a Midsummer celebration, but not everyone is able to dance around a bonfire. Use this candle spell instead to get some of that same power and energy.

You will need a medium-sized cauldron or a fire-safe bowl, sand or salt, and seven small tapers. Beeswax tapers are best, if you can find them, but any candle will do. Candles that are red, orange, yellow, or a combination of those colors make for an extra energetic spell. You will also need four pieces of red or orange ribbon. Two should be long enough to tie around an ankle with a small bit left over to flutter as you move. The other two may be tied into a loose circle that you can slide over your hands and then tighten one-handed, if you are doing this alone.

This is a simple spell that mimics the larger blaze of a bonfire, for those who can't have one. For full effect, the spell should be done at dusk or dark, when the light from the candle flames will shine out into the darkness. This can be done outside or inside.

Place the cauldron or dish on the ground/floor/low altar and fill it about three-quarters full with sand. If you don't have sand, salt will do. Set the seven candles securely into the sand, making sure that they won't fall over. Place the four pieces of ribbon in front of the cauldron. If possible, locate the cauldron/dish in an area surrounded by enough space that you can dance around it safely.

As the sun is setting, say:

It is Midsummer! The sun is filled with power and energy!

Light the candles. As you light each one, say:

> *Midsummer sun, share your power with me!*
> *Midsummer sun, share your energy with me!*

Once all the candles are lit, spend a minute gazing at their brightness. Feel their warmth, like the warmth of the sun. If you want, you can even close your eyes and envision a huge bonfire surrounded by dancing witches. When you're ready, open your eyes and pick up the pieces of ribbon. Hold them a safe distance above the flames, raised up in both hands in front of you, and say:

> *Into these ribbons I call the energy of the flame!*
> *Into these ribbons I call the power of the sun!*

Tie one ribbon around each ankle and each wrist, and feel that energy and power moving into you. If you can, dance or move around the cauldron, taking in even more of that energy. Otherwise, simply stand in front of the candles and feel your body vibrate with the energy of the solstice.

When you are done, say:

I thank you, flames, for all you have given me.
Your fire and your light are a gift that is truly appreciated.
I thank you, Midsummer sun, for the power and energy
you bring to the earth, now shared with me and truly appreciated.

Snuff out the candles. If you want, you can wear or carry one or all of the ribbons when you need a boost of energy or to feel empowered.

Green and Growing Herbal Prosperity (Earth Spell)

Midsummer is the perfect time to do prosperity work by tapping into the energy of abundance and growth that is all around us. You can choose whichever herbs or greenery appeal to you, as long as they are plants that are at their peak. I like to use fast-growing herbs, such as thyme, parsley, and basil—if you really want to pull their power into you, toss them into your dinner after you're done with your magickal work.

You will need three or four kinds of herbs or green plants, a green pillar candle, and a fire-safe plate to put the candle and herbs on. You will also need small bowls of salt and water, a sage smudge stick or some incense, an athame or small pointed object to draw on the candle with (a toothpick works fine), and an empty bowl or cauldron.

The best time to do this spell is at noon, outside under the bright sun, but other times of day or inside are okay if they are necessary. Carve the rune symbol for *Fehu* ᚠ on the candle. You can also carve an equal-armed cross, a spiral, a wheel, or any other Midsummer symbols you like. Set the candle in the middle of the plate, sticking it down by dripping a little wax onto the plate if you need to. Place the herbs neatly around the edges of the plate.

Light the candle and say:

> *I call down the power of the Midsummer sun to energize*
> *my magickal work with the element of fire.*

Sprinkle the herbs with a bit of salt and say:

> *I call upon the element of earth to energize my magickal work*
> *and bless these plants that sprang from its fertile soil.*

Sprinkle the herbs with a bit of water and say:

*I call upon the element of water to energize my magickal work
as the rains empower the growing things in the fields and meadows.*

Light the sage or incense and waft it over the herbs, saying:

*As the winds blow the pollen and fertilize the world,
let them blow prosperity and abundance to me.*

Take up some of each kind of herb and hold them in your hand. Feel their energy vibrating between your fingers and crush them slightly so that their aroma rises up toward the summer sun. Then say this spell:

*Herbs and plants, sun and light,
empowered by Midsummer's glow.
Green to green, gold so bright,
let prosperity flow.
So mote it be.*

Place the herbs you are holding into the empty bowl and either leave them on your altar, or out in the sunlight, or use them to cook with (if they are edible).

Because there is one spell for each of the elements, if you *really* want to make the most of the Midsummer energy, you can do an all-day ritual, incorporating all four spells into your day. Start at dawn with Greet the Dawn (Air Spell), do the Healing Water Spell either midmorning or midafternoon, the Green and Growing Herbal Prosperity Spell at noon, and then finish out the day at sundown with the Fire Power Candle Magick. If you are doing a vigil and going from dawn to dawn, the fire spell can be used to end things at dawn on the second day.

More Midsummer Spells

Here are a few other Midsummer spells for you to try out:

Thor's Summer Storm Spell

There are a number of storm/lightning/rain gods associated with Midsummer in various cultures. This is probably due, at least in part, to the fact that rain is just as important to raising successful crops as the sun is. Even today, with modern irrigation to assist them, farmers are at the mercy of the weather. Too little rain and the crops won't grow tall and strong. Too much rain at the wrong time and everything in the fields may be ruined. There is little wonder that earlier cultures prayed to the gods that controlled the weather.

A good storm will wash away debris, clear the air of pollen, and generally refresh the land. Big enough storms can actually change the landscape. Most of us could use a good clearing and cleansing from time to time. And sometimes we need to create an internal storm to help push us through a time of change. If it happens to be raining on or around Midsummer, you can try this spell to call on Thor's help.

If it is raining gently enough, it is nice to do this spell standing outside, even if you get wet. If there is thunder and lightning, though, it is best to talk to Thor from the safety of inside your house or on a covered porch. If you can't be outside, try opening a window so that you can hear the rain, and maybe stick a hand out into it.

Thor was associated not just with thunder, but also strength, the oak tree, and healing. He is fiercely protective and known for his powerful magickal hammer. Thursday is actually named for Thor's Day. So you might want to do this spell on a Thursday if you can't do it on Midsummer.

You will need an offering for Thor. Mead or ale are the usual ones, but you can put out a bowl of some hearty stew, a chunk of meat, or even some honey. You will also need a bowl to gather rainwater in (if you can't get to the rain or there isn't any, just use whatever water you have) and a towel to dry off with. If you are going to be outside in the rain, you may want to print out the spell and put it in a plastic bag so it will stay dry enough to read.

This is an extremely simple spell. It is more about connection and your intentions than anything else. The spell should be said with feeling and with as much focus as you can muster.

Walk out into the rain or stand by the window so you can hear the rain coming down. Place the offering on the ground in front of you (or nearby, if you are inside). Place the empty bowl on the ground so it can fill with water. Lift your arms and say:

Great Thor, god of the thunder, hear me!
Great Thor, protector and warrior, hear me!
Great Thor, who brings the healing rain, hear me!
Let your rain wash down upon me, cleansing and clearing.
Let your mighty thunder shake the skies and the ground,
bringing positive change in my life.
Let the summer storm bring me new life and new beginnings,
and help me to grow strong and tall like the oak.
Thor, lend me your power and strength,
and bless me with the rains of this summer storm.

Gather up the bowl and take it inside, use the towel to dry off. The bowl of water can be placed on your altar or some other safe place, and you can use it in your magickal work over the coming days and weeks, or whenever you feel that you need a boost. If you can't be outside, you can stick your bowl out the window, or simply send the energy you gathered into a bowl of regular water. If you can, leave your offering out for a while.

Crystal Spell for Courage, Protection, and Strength

Many of the gemstones associated with Midsummer are thought to have the qualities of protection, strength, and increasing courage. Three in particular—citrine, carnelian, and tiger-eye—are powerful stones that are also relatively inexpensive and easy to find. Citrine often comes in the form of a cut crystal, while you are more likely to see carnelian and tiger-eye as tumbled stones. Either form works equally well for this spell, and you can use all three or just one, depending on what you happen to have.

If possible, do this spell outside in the sunlight at noon on Midsummer's Day. It will work fine if you can't, of course—this is just the time when it will be the most powerful, since the spell is drawing on the power of the sun at its zenith.

You need gemstone(s) of your choice and a small square piece of yellow, orange, or red fabric, about three inches by three inches (it can be smaller or larger depending on the size of your stones), and a piece of ribbon or yarn to tie around the cloth. You will also need an acorn or an oak leaf, or a piece of paper cut out in the shape of an oak leaf to represent the oak. If you would like, you can also use a piece of paper with the word courage, protection, and/or strength written on it, depending on what you need the most help with. If you want to be able to hang the finished bag around your neck, substitute a piece of leather or silk cord for the ribbon, or make the ribbon longer.

Sit outside at noon on Midsummer. Place all of the supplies on a plate or a tray in front of you. Close your eyes for a moment and feel the power of the sun on your face. Pick up your stone or crystal(s) and hold them out in your open palm, so the sun can shine on them. Say:

> *Midsummer sun so strong, send me your strength and power.*
> *Help me to shine brightly and be filled with courage.*
> *Help me to stand strong and proud.*
> *Protect me, and help me to protect myself.*
> *Let me shine like the sun, and be strong like the oak,*
> *and let these stones absorb your energy so they might*
> *lend it to me when I need it. So mote it be.*

Place the stones with the oak representation in the middle of the cloth, and tie the ribbon or cord around it. Hold it up to the sun one more time, and then take a moment to hold it close to your heart while visualizing yourself as strong, brave, and protected by a shining yellow light.

You can now wear the bag around your neck, if you choose. You can also carry your stone with you or place it on your altar or under your pillow.

Folk Divination

There are many forms of "folk" divination for Midsummer that can be found in the traditions of various cultures. Probably the best known is using a daisy for simple love divination, by plucking out its petals one by one and saying, "He loves me, he loves me not, he loves me, he loves me not." Whichever one you landed on last was supposed to be the truth. How many of us did that as kids and maybe even as adults?

Love divination was probably the most common on Midsummer. Daisies featured in another standard divination, in which a girl (these were almost always done by girls or women) went into a field where daisies grew, closed her eyes, and grabbed a handful of grass and flowers. However many daisies she pulled up would indicate how many years would pass before she married.

One superstition said that if you took the flowers from beneath an oak tree on Midsummer Eve and tucked them under your pillow, you would dream of the person you would marry.

A Welsh tradition said that if you washed your clothes at a well at midnight, and chanted: "He who would be my partner, let him come and wash with me," then your lover would come and help you with the laundry. (Franklin, 45) Seems like a reasonable way to pick a future mate to me. At least you know he cleans!

Modern Divination

Tarot

For something a little more up-to-date, you can do this Summer Solstice tarot spread I created. It is quite simple, so don't worry if you're not a tarot-reading pro.

Shuffle the cards while thinking of your question or issue. Then, lay out six cards in a circle with their ends pointing out so the spread looks like a sun. The cards should be placed all at once, facing down, and then turned up one by one.

The bottom card represents you or the person the reading is for. The next card to the left represents the situation or your question. Continuing around the circle (sunwise, of course), the following cards represent the obstacles that stand in your way, possible solutions to those obstacles, guidance or suggestions to give you direction, and then finally, the future card, to the right of the card you started out with.

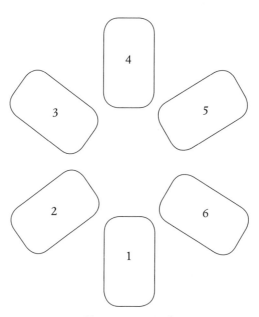

Tarot sun spread

You may want to begin by saying a small prayer for help and guidance, and then finish by saying thank you. It is particularly appropriate to do this reading outside at noon on Midsummer, if that is possible.

Three Rune Reading

Runes are simple to work with. They are very popular with some of the Germanic and Norse cultures that considered Midsummer to be one of the most important holidays of the year.

For an easy Summer Solstice divination with rune stones, pull three runes without looking. The first one you put down will represent the year behind you (so far), the second the present day, and the third, the remainder of the current year. You can either ask a question of the runes before you pull them, such as "Will I find love this year?", or just wait and see what comes up.

Dream Divination

Two of the herbs associated with Midsummer, mugwort and lavender, are also herbs that have been used for centuries to encourage prophetic dreams. You can place some of each in a small drawstring bag or sachet, and add a bit of chamomile if you like, for good sleep. If you have a question, you can write it down on a slip of paper and put it into the bag along with the herbs or ask it aloud as you lie down in bed. Tuck the bag under your pillow, and perhaps you will dream of the answer.

Herbal Spells and Charms

Here are some general suggestions for herbs that are associated with Midsummer and ways that you might use them in your spellwork, divining, and other modes of celebrating the holiday.

Chamomile: A healing herb that was sacred to various sun gods, including Ra (Egyptian), Cernunnos (Celtic), and Balder (Norse). Make an offering of chamomile tea, or throw some of the small white flowers into the Midsummer bonfire. Chamomile is known for its calming properties, so if you have issues with anxiety or stress, you can harvest chamomile on Midsummer and dry for use later.

Cinnamon: This spicy bark has long been used for love magick, to increase energy, and for prosperity work—all themes that come into play on Midsummer. Put a stick of cinnamon on your altar in honor of the gods and goddesses of love, or use cinnamon in your cakes and ale for your rituals. Cinnamon can also be used in the form of incense. A small handful of powdered cinnamon can be thrown on the fire as well.

Daisy: Associated with the Summer Solstice because of its resemblance to the sun, with white rays coming out from the yellow center, the daisy is sacred to many sun gods. It represents both love and innocence. It is said that daisies picked between noon and one o'clock on Midsummer (when the sun is high) have especially magickal qualities.

Elder: The elder is sacred to many goddesses. Elderflowers and elderberries are used to make tea and jam and to flavor mead. The berries are used medicinally for their immune-boosting properties. Birds love the berries, so if you have space to plant an elderberry bush or two, plan to share. Put out some berries or flowers to attract the faeries.

Foxglove: Foxglove is one of the herbs said to attract faeries. Once called "Witch's Bells," perhaps because of its common use in magick. In England, the flowers were sometimes put around sacred wells. However, foxglove is poisonous, and should only be grown for decorative purposes.

Hazel: Sacred to the Celtic god Lugh and to faeries, hazel is often used as a divining rod to find water or treasure. Hazel nuts were traditionally eaten to increase fertility.

Heather: Bees are attracted to the flowers of this low-growing shrub, making it one of the special Midsummer plants. If the blossoms are made into a tea, it is said to act as a general tonic. Heather is sacred to the goddess Cybele.

Lavender: It is traditional to throw a handful of lavender flowers into the Midsummer bonfire, in honor of the gods and goddesses (especially love goddesses), and for peace in the year to come. Lavender is an herb often used both medicinally and magickally for peace, healing, and sleep. Lavender incense can be burned to attract the faeries or to purify your ritual circle. Lavender is also used for love magick.

Marigold: Marigold is another "sun" flower, since its bright yellows and oranges look like small suns, and one of its folk names is "summer's bride." If they are picked at noon, marigolds are said to strengthen and comfort the heart. Marigolds can be strung into garlands and are often used at Hindu weddings and to decorate their altars. If you are going to be having a handfasting at Midsummer, you may want to string some marigolds together. Medicinally, marigold is often used topically to treat wounds and bruises.

Meadowsweet: Meadowsweet is one of the Druid's most sacred herbs, also known as "Queen of the Meadow" and "Lady of the Meadow," and sometimes called "Bridewort" because of its use in weddings. Meadowsweet is sacred to many goddesses, including Aine (Celtic) and Venus (Roman).

Mistletoe: The folk names for mistletoe include "Thunderbesom" and "Witches Broom." It was sacred to the Druids, who cut it on Midsummer. Lore says that if you are going to cut it, to try not to let it hit the ground, and use only one stroke of the knife to sever it. Mistletoe found growing on an oak was supposed to be the most powerful. Legend also has it that if you kiss your beloved under the mistletoe, your love will last forever.

Mugwort: Ironically known both as *Artemis Herb (or Artemisia)* and St. John's Plant, Mugwort is a powerful herb for magick to increase psychic ability, lucid dreaming, and divination. If you are going to be doing divination work on Midsummer, you can burn mugwort in the bonfire, use it as incense, or make a magickal wash to be placed on mirrors, crystal balls, or other scrying tools. A small pillow or sachet filled with mugwort and placed by the pillow is said to aid in both dreaming and astral projection.

Oak: The most sacred tree of the Druids, prized in other cultures as well, such as the Greeks, who had sacred oak groves. Often associated with thunder gods, in part because oaks are supposedly more likely to be struck by lightning than any other trees. They live for hundreds (perhaps thousands) of years, with strong, deep roots and branches that reach up into the sky. It was traditional to use oak wood on the Midsummer bonfires. In the ancient Ogham secret alphabet developed by the Druids, the oak was called *duir,* and stood for power, strength, Midsummer, and doorways. For a Midsummer ritual, you can use oak in the form of wood, leaves, or acorns.

Rose: Sacred to many love goddesses and also used as a symbol for the sun, roses can be placed on the altar, or used in Midsummer charms for love. Scatter the petals around the edges of your circle to enclose it, especially if you are doing a handfasting ritual. A tea can be made out of rose hips and used for cakes and ale, or left out for the faeries. It can also be sipped before bed if you want to dream of love.

Rosemary: The faeries are said to be fond of this herb, so you can use it if you are trying to attract the Fae folk. Traditionally used at weddings and handfastings, and also in love magick. A powerfully protective herb, it can also be thrown in the bonfire, used in incense, or scattered around a sacred circle. Try baking bread or cakes with rosemary in it to serve at your feast.

Rowan: It is traditional to make a protection charm from rowan wood tied with a red thread; hang this up if you are concerned about visits from unwelcome visitors on Midsummer. Rowan can also be used to help attract spirits or spirit guides. Rowan is either a tree or a shrub, and one of its folk names is witchwood, due to its common use in divining rods. It has long been associated with witches, and they are often found planted near stone circles.

St. John's Wort: This is one of the herbs particularly associated with Midsummer, which is considered the best time to harvest it. It has golden flowers that represent the sun and fire. It is said to bleed red when cut, the sap is referred to as St. John's blood. Traditionally it was used for healing and to banish darkness and negativity. It was called *beathnua* (life-renewer) by the Irish and considered highly protective.

Interestingly, modern herbalists commonly use St. John's Wort to treat depression. Gather it at noon on Midsummer for extra healing power, or throw it into the fire (inside or outside) to protect the home.

Vervain: Vervain is not to be confused with lemon verbena, which is a completely different plant, despite vervain's Latin name of *Verbena Officialis.* One of the special magickal herbs of Midsummer, Vervain has long been associated with witches. Some of its folk names include "Enchanter's Plant," "Juno's Tears," and "Simpler's Joy." (A simpler is one who makes simples, or herbal remedies.) Lore has it that it is best to collect your yearly supply of vervain on Midsummer, and any left from the previous year should be thrown on the bonfire. It is sacred to a number of love goddesses, moon goddesses, and thunder gods, and it is used both for love magick and to protect the home from lightning.

Yarrow: Another one of the herbs specifically associated with Midsummer, yarrow can be tossed on the bonfire as an offering to the gods or used for love, healing, or protection magick.

A note on herbs: some people are sensitive to various plants, including herbs. All herbs should be used with caution until you are certain you have no issues with them. Just because something is natural doesn't mean it can't hurt you.

RECIPES
AND
CRAFTS

beginnings, birth, renewal, rejuvenation, balance, fertility, change

strength, vernal equinox, sun enters Aries, Libra in the Heav

Green Man, Amalthea, Aphrodite, Blodeuwedd, Eostre, Ea

Flora, Freya, Gaia, Guinevere, Persephone, Libera, M

npet, Umaj, Vila, Aengus MacOg, Cernunnos, Herma, The

ama, Mabon Osiris, Pan, Thor, abundance, growth, health, ca

l healing, patience understanding virtue, spring, honor, contentme

hic abilities, spiritual truth, intuition, receptivity, love, inner se

rovement, spiritual awareness, purification, childhood, innocence,

ty, creativity, communication, concentration, divination, harmon

bilities, prosperity, attraction, blessings, happiness, luck, money,

, guidance, visions, insight, family, wishes, celebrating life cyc

endship, courage, attracts love, honesty, good health, emotions,

improvement, influence, motivation, peace, rebirth, self preserva

mine power, freedom, optimism, new beginnings, vernal equinox

creation, sun, apple blossom, columbine, crocus, daffodil, daisy,

sy, honeysuckle, jasmine, jonquil, lilac, narcissus, orange blossom

rose, rose, the fool, the magician, the priestess, justice, the star

, gathering, growth, abundance, eggs, seeds, honey, dill, asparag

*E*VERY HOLIDAY HAS its own themes, colors, and energy, and those things are used not only for spells and rituals, but also in choosing recipes to serve at our sabbat meals or feasts, in coming up with craft ideas, and inspiring us as we decorate our homes and altars.

You don't have to celebrate with a large group, or even be out of the broom closet, in order to make use of some of these ideas. This is particularly true at Midsummer, when much of the decor or craft possibilities can simply be seen as getting into the swing of summer.

Midsummer Recipes

It can be fun to host a Summer Solstice picnic or barbecue and invite family and friends to enjoy it with you. After all, Midsummer is all about the celebration of summer, so if you are a solitary witch, you can have the best of both worlds by sharing the celebration with others, and then honoring the day with a private ritual of your own when everyone else goes home.

If you are fortunate enough to have some like-minded Pagan folks to observe Litha with, you can have a group ritual followed by a glorious Midsummer potluck feast. Invite everyone to bring their favorite summer-themed dishes, created out of the fresh fruits and vegetables so readily available at this time of year, along with some bread to represent the wheat in the fields. If you're *really* lucky, maybe someone will bring some homemade mead or strawberry wine.

If feasting with others, please be mindful of food allergies and alcohol issues. For a larger potluck, ask each person to make up a card with the ingredients of their dish that can be placed near it. That way anyone with food sensitivities will know exactly what they can eat and what to avoid.

Summer Abundance Salad

Salads don't have to be boring, and there is nothing better than fresh greens, ripe tomatoes, and other typical salad ingredients when they are moments out of the garden, still warm from the summer sun. If you don't have a garden, try getting as many of your salad ingredients as you can from a local farmer's market or farm stand. Organic is always best if you can find it and afford it. This salad has the added bonus of using many ingredients that are good for abundance and prosperity magick, so if you want, you can make this salad magickal by focusing on those Midsummer themes while putting the salad together.

Ingredients:

Lettuce and other greens, torn into bite-sized pieces

Fresh herbs—some of the best at this time of year include
    basil, parsley, mint, dill, and/or chives

Fresh fruit—strawberries, pomegranate seeds, peaches,
    or melon

Sunflower seeds

Vinaigrette made with olive oil and balsamic vinegar, or other
    salad dressings

Shredded Parmesan cheese (optional)

Gather lettuce and other greens including spinach, baby kale, and some arugula or mustard greens for a little extra bite. Sprinkle in fresh herbs from the options above. Remember that mint is strong and should be used sparingly. Add fruit to the salad, which gives a touch of sweetness that contrasts nicely with the slight bitterness of some of the greens and herbs. Just try to use fruits that are in season and available locally. Then, sprinkle sunflower seeds on top of your salad to add nutrition and interest, as well as the perfect representation of the sun. Finally, drizzle vinaigrette or salad dressing on top. If you like, add Parmesan cheese to finish the salad.

Couscous Celebration Salad

Cold dishes are wonderfully refreshing on a hot summer day. This one is extremely simple and easy to throw together, and is suitable for vegetarians and young cooks. Couscous is a tiny Middle Eastern pasta that cooks in five minutes. Once it cools, it can be fluffed with a fork and makes a fun platform for the fresh veggies and herbs. Other types of pasta can be substituted, especially if you can find them in fun, summery shapes.

Ingredients:

1 to 2 cups of dry couscous

1 to 2 cups of water

1 or 2 large tomatoes, chopped small, or ½ pound to 1 pound of grape tomatoes

2 small cucumbers, chopped into small pieces

Small bunch of fresh mint, torn or cut into small pieces

¼ cup olive oil

Salt and pepper to taste

Lemon juice to taste

Cook the couscous according to the directions on the package. Make 1 to 2 cups of dry couscous depending on how many people you will be feeding. When the couscous has cooled, toss tomatoes, cucumbers, mint, and olive oil with it and allow the mixture to sit for at least half an hour for the flavors to blend together. If desired, add salt, pepper, and lemon juice before serving.

Summer Solstice Salsa

Salsa is extremely easy to make, and you can vary the ingredients to suit your tastes. It's so simple, you might want to make one mild one and one that is hot to reflect the heat of the summer sun. The fresher the tomatoes, the better the salsa tastes.

Ingredients:

4 to 6 large tomatoes (for a really colorful salsa, use some red tomatoes and some yellow and/or orange ones)

1 small sweet onion or red onion, chopped fine

1 small cucumber, chopped fine (optional)

1 to 2 cloves of garlic, mashed and chopped fine

1 small hot pepper

1 to 2 tablespoons of chopped parsley or cilantro (cilantro is traditional, but about 50 percent of the population perceives it to have a bitter or soapy taste, so if you're not sure everyone likes it, you may want to use parsley)

Salt and pepper to taste

Squeeze of lemon to add brightness

Peaches (optional)

Tortilla chips or homemade flatbread

Chop tomatoes into small pieces. Mix in chopped onion, cucumber, and garlic. Add chopped pepper. Use only a small amount of a mild pepper for mild salsa, or use a hotter pepper for really spicy stuff—the seeds contain much of the heat, so leave them out if you don't want your salsa to have as much punch. Toss in the parsley or cilantro, salt, pepper, and lemon. If you like, add some cut up peaches for a touch of sweetness. Let the salsa sit for at least an hour. Serve with sturdy tortilla chips or homemade flatbread.

Ale for the Gods Bread

Ale is often used as an offering for some of the gods who are celebrated at Midsummer. Breaking bread together is also a tradition in many cultures. This is a fast and easy bread made with ale and only a few other ingredients. You can eat it with your meal, or pass it around the circle and have everyone pull off a piece during cakes and ale.

Ingredients:
3 cups flour
3 teaspoons baking powder
1 ½ teaspoons salt
2 tablespoons sugar
12 ounce bottle of ale
½ cup butter, melted
Dried dill (optional)

Preheat oven to 350°F. Mix all dry ingredients together and slowly add in ale, stirring clockwise. Put batter into three 6 inch x 3 inch loaf pans or two larger ones. Drizzle the butter on top of the loaf and sprinkle with dill if desired. Bake for 50 minutes or until toothpick comes out dry. (Adapted from Wood and Seefeldt)

Fruit Soup #1: Melon Madness

We rarely think to make soup from fruit, but there is nothing that celebrates the summer better than a chilled fruit soup. As an added benefit, there is no cooking when it is hot!

Ingredients:

1 mango, peeled and sliced

1 small melon (any kind except watermelon), seeded and cut small

Juice from 1 orange (about ¼ cup)

½ teaspoon to 2 teaspoons sugar or honey

Fresh raspberries—about a cup

2 tablespoons Gran Marnier or any raspberry flavored liquor, such as Chambord (optional)

Edible flowers to decorate the top of the soup (optional)

Puree the mango, melon, and orange juice in a blender until smooth. You may need to do this in a few batches. Taste and sweeten slightly with sugar or honey if necessary. The soup should not be too sweet. Rinse blender and then puree raspberries and a small amount of sugar or honey. Start with ½ teaspoon and add more until it is at the desired sweetness. If desired, add liquor and blend. Place melon mixture and raspberries in separate bowls and chill for at least 2 hours. Serve either in one large bowl or small individual bowls by placing melon soup in bowl, then gently swirling raspberry mixture on top. Sprinkle with edible flowers if using. (Adapted from Wood and Seefeldt)

Fruit Soup #2: Cherries Jubilation

This soup is made with cherries, so if they happen to be ripe when you celebrate Midsummer, you're in luck! This soup's vibrant color and sweet flavor seem to capture the essence of summer in a bowl.

Ingredients:
2 ½ pounds sweet cherries, pitted
¼ cup honey or maple syrup
4 cups water
1 small lemon, juiced with skin zested and reserved
Whipped cream or sour cream

Combine cherries and sweetener in a pot with water, bring to a boil, and then simmer for 20 minutes. Let cool, then blend with lemon juice in a blender or food processor until smooth. Pour into a main bowl or individual serving bowls. If you want, you can add a few more cherries, chopped fine, or some of the lemon zest. Offer whipped cream or sour cream for people to dollop on top if desired. (Adapted from Johnson)

Bountiful Beets Baked with Orange

Root vegetables spend their growing time under the ground, pulling in nutrition from the soil and energy from the sun by way of aboveground leaves. Beet greens are edible, especially when young, so if you are buying fresh beets with the green tops still attached, don't throw them away; eat them! Beets are perfect Midsummer feast food—they have all that earth energy stored up inside them, and their beautiful color is just right for a feast shared with friends.

Ingredients:

12 medium beets (fewer if the beets are large—you can also use orange beets instead of red ones, to bring a more sunny color into the dish)

2 oranges

Salt and pepper to taste

Fresh rosemary

Orange slices for garnish (optional)

Preheat the oven to 350°F. Clean beets and peel them (if the beets are organic, and have relatively thin skin, you can skip the peeling). Cut into slices. Grate the zest of one of the oranges, then juice them both. Lay the beet slices overlapping each other in an ovenproof pan or dish, pour orange juice over the top, then sprinkle with zest, salt, and pepper. You can either chop up a bit of rosemary and sprinkle it on top, or place the whole sprigs on top of the dish. Roast in oven for about 1 hour, or until tender. Decorate with orange slices if desired when serving.

Leg of Lamb with Herb Rub

Our ancestors almost always celebrated Midsummer with some form of meat, often roasting whole oxen, goats, or other animals, depending on the size of the crowd they were serving. This may seem cruel to some modern folks, but for those who lived on the land, death was simply a part of the cycle of life. The animals were often offered up as a sacrifice to the gods in thanks for the bounty of the season, and then every part of the animal was used, from the roast on the spit to the bones, which might have been carved into tools or decorations, or made into soup after the feast was over. If you are serving meat of some sort at your Midsummer meal (whether it is an entire roast or ham sandwiches), offer up a piece to the gods and eat it with gratitude and appreciation for the animal that gave up its life so that you might live.

Note: This herb rub is suitable for any strongly favored meat—if you don't want to make lamb, it will work as well on beef or pork. The amount of garlic may seem overwhelming, but because the roast cooks slowly, the garlic is roasted until it is nutty and sweet. Fresh herbs are wonderful at this time of year, but you can use dried if that is all you have.

Ingredients:

Large or medium roast

1 tablespoon dried oregano (use double if fresh)

1 tablespoon dried rosemary or 1 large sprig of fresh
rosemary

1 tablespoon dried thyme (if you can find lemon thyme, it is
especially nice) or 2 tablespoons if fresh

2 tablespoons sea salt (coarse kosher salt is okay)

Ground pepper to taste

12 cloves of garlic, peeled, smashed, and chopped small (if
you're doing the rub in a food processer, you can just cut
into a couple of pieces, and the machine will do the rest)

¼ cup olive oil

Prepare the roast and place on a roasting rack if you have one. This can also be done on a barbecue rotisserie if you can keep the temperature low enough. Combine herbs, garlic, salt, and pepper in a blender or food processer. Blend until you have a reasonably smooth paste, and then smear over the surface area of the roast.

For leg of lamb, cook in 325°F oven, allowing 35 minutes per pound (it may take longer if you are using bone-in leg). Meat should read 140°F on a thermometer for rare, 160°F for medium. The coating will have formed a lovely fragrant crust. Allow to sit for at least 10 to 15 minutes before slicing.

Rosemary Shortbread Cookies

These make a nice "cake" for cakes and ale, or a light desert at the end of a summer picnic. Rosemary is good for remembrance, so eat these on an occasion you would like to hold in your heart and mind forever, such as a handfasting or a wedding!

Ingredients:

1 cup butter

1 cup sugar

3 cups flour (reserve ½ cup)

3 to 4 tablespoons finely chopped rosemary (use less if the rosemary is fresh instead of dried)

Preheat oven to 275°F. Cream butter and sugar together. Add 2 ½ cups flour and the rosemary. Mix well. Flour your workspace with reserved flour and turn dough out onto surface. Knead until dough begins to crack, then roll out until it is ¼ inch thick. You can cut it into rectangles, or cut out fancy shapes like suns. Bake on ungreased cookie sheets until lightly browned, about 50 minutes.

Chocolate Tomato Cake

No one will guess the secret ingredient in this cake, but the addition of green tomatoes (prevalent at this time of year) will give it a summery boost. The recipe also contains other Midsummer ingredients, including cinnamon and orange peel.

Ingredients:

2 ½ cups flour

½ cup cocoa

2 ½ teaspoons baking powder

2 teaspoons baking soda

1 teaspoon salt

1 teaspoon cinnamon

¾ cup butter

2 cups sugar

3 eggs

2 teaspoons vanilla

2 teaspoons grated orange peel (more to garnish, if desired)

2 cups green tomatoes, coarsely grated

1 cup walnuts, finely chopped

½ cup milk

Powdered sugar or frosting of your choice

Preheat oven to 350°F. Combine dry ingredients and set aside. Cream butter and sugar, then add eggs one at a time, beating in well. Stir in vanilla, orange peel, and tomatoes and mix with a wooden spoon. Add nuts, then add dry mixture to wet mixture, alternating with the milk. When well combined, bake in a greased pan for about one hour. Let cool in the pan for 15 minutes, then turn upside down onto serving plate.

To serve, dust with powdered sugar and sprinkle with orange peel, or top with the frosting of your choice.

Midsummer Fruited Wine

There all sorts of beverages you can serve at an outside picnic or feast, but few are as summery as sangria. Sangria is a typical Spanish and Portuguese treat made from wine, fruit, and some form of sweetener, sometimes with a bit of brandy added as well. Americanized versions sometimes replace the brandy with some kind of bubbly soda, such as ginger ale, Sprite, or 7UP. (Personally, I suggest you reserve that for the kid's non-alcoholic version.) You can experiment with the ingredients until you find a combination you enjoy. I like to think of sangria as the perfect libation to offer the gods on Midsummer because of its combination of wine and fruit. If you are eating outside, you may want to put a small amount in a bowl for the faeries as well. This is just their kind of thing.

Ingredients:

1 bottle of red wine (a good medium table wine is best for this—nothing too sweet or too dry)

1 orange, sliced

1 lemon, sliced

½ cup strawberries, sliced

Honey to taste (don't make it too sweet)

Freeze some fruit in ice trays ahead of time (cut up fruit or berries in a small amount of water, and/or lemon or orange peel) (optional)

Grape juice, for a nonalcoholic kids version (also good for any guests who are avoiding alcohol, or the designated drivers) (optional)

If possible, use a clear pitcher for this, so people can see how beautiful it is. Pour wine into the container, add sliced fruit, and add honey to taste. If using fruited ice cubes, add those right before the sangria is put out on the table. A nonalcoholic version can be made with grape juice instead of wine. Make sure you use bright purple juice, not white grape juice, which doesn't have the same jewel tones.

Midsummer Crafts

Whether you are celebrating Midsummer by yourself, with friends, or with your children, crafts are one way to add a fun element to the holiday while also focusing on the themes and traditions that go along with the season. Many cultures had particular crafts and activities associated with the Summer Solstice, and these are a few easy updated versions to get you in the Midsummer mood.

Sunshine Wreaths

Wreaths were traditional in a number of different cultures and were usually created by women. The wreaths were either worn like crowns on top of the head or thrown into lakes, streams, or oceans. In one country, women would make wreaths and then watch the sun come up while looking through them. Men occasionally wore wreaths made from oak leaves, too.

You can either make a wreath to wear, to hang up as a decoration, or to toss into water, if you happen to have some nearby. How you are going to use your finished product may influence your choice of wreath base, but everything else will remain the same. Remember that if you are throwing your wreath into water (other than your own swimming pool, at least), all parts of it should be rapidly biodegradable. You will need the following supplies:

- Wreath base—this can be grapevine (thinner if you will be wearing it, thicker for decoration) or florist's wire (this is a coated wire this would work well for a circlet) or any flexible natural vine/supple branch (like willow). If you are really good at weaving together flower stems, you can even dispense with a base altogether. You can often find a wreath base in the craft section of stores. Just make sure you are using natural materials (no Styrofoam, for instance).

- Flowers—you can use all one kind, or various different types and colors. The focus here is on rayed flowers that represent the sun, such as daisies, marigolds, sunflowers, carnations, and such. You can also use roses, chamomile, St. John's Wort, and even ferns for accents. For a truly wild look, add dandelions. Try for bright yellows, oranges, and reds.

- Ribbons—you can use whatever thickness you like; you will probably want thinner ribbons to wear and thicker ones for hanging wreaths. Again, you can choose one color, but it will be fancier with a few different ones. Try to get ribbon that goes with the colors of your flowers, although you can also add white, gold, or any other summery accent colors. The length of ribbon will depend on how you are using it, and how big the wreath will be, but you will probably need at least a yard or two of each color, maybe more.

- Scissors
- Glue or tape (optional)

Wreaths are quite simple to make, although it may take some fiddling to get yours just right. Wind the grapevine or wire into a circle that will fit your head comfortably (if wearing), or about the size you want for a decorative piece, remembering that it will look larger once you have added the flowers. Wind the material around itself so it stays in place, or fasten it together with ribbon or glue. Tuck flowers in one at a time, winding the stems in and out to keep them in place. If you want, wind ribbon(s) in and out around the circle of the wreath as well. Try to make the finished piece look balanced (alternate colors, for instance) and neat, but don't worry too much about perfection! If necessary, you can use a dab of glue here and there to keep things in place. If desired, you can dangle a number of ribbons from the back (circlet) or bottom (decorative).

Alternately, if your flowers have long enough stems, you can simply wind, tuck, or braid them together. This is especially nice if you are going to be tossing the wreath on the water.

Viking Boats
In some cultures, Midsummer is celebrated by making small boats, filling them with offerings, and placing them on lakes, streams, or the ocean. If you want to get fancy, you can go on-line and find fairly easy instructions for making origami Viking

boats. But there is also a way to make a little raft-type boat that is simple enough to do with even the smallest child. If you don't have a body of water nearby, you can float these in a pool or a large bowl. You will need:

- 9 wooden Popsicle sticks (you can find these in the craft section of many stores)
- 1 tall stick, 8 to 12 inches long (a wooden barbecue skewer works well, or you can actually use a thin, lightweight stick)
- Piece of colorful paper (any kind) to use as a sail
- Small piece of cork (cut off the bottom of a wine cork, or look for cork rounds that protect floors from being scratched)
- White glue
- Lightweight flowers or flower petals
- Marker or pens (optional)

The idea here is to make a simple boat that you will place your offerings on and "sail" into the sunset (or dawn, if you prefer). For kids, it is probably enough to just make the boat. For adults, you may want to add the magickal touch of writing your wishes for the season on the pieces of Popsicle stick—prosperity, healing, love, etc. If you're doing this, write your words before you start assembling the boat.

Take six of your sticks and lay them out next to each other, so they look like a small raft. Glue the remaining three sticks across two ends and the middle of the raft, to hold them all together.

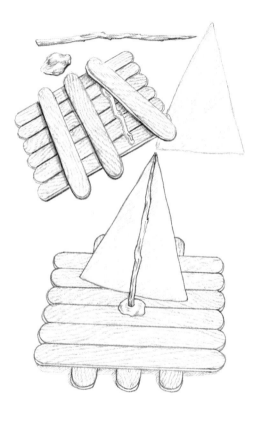

Once these have dried, turn your raft over so the support sticks are on the bottom. Glue your piece of cork to the middle of the boat.

Cut a piece of your paper into a triangle (the sail) and glue it to the top edge of your stick. Then push the bottom of the stick into the cork or clay, using glue if necessary to hold it steady.

Your boat is now finished. You can place the flower petals on it and set it on the water, sending it out into the Midsummer dawn or dusk.

Cinnamon Brooms

Cinnamon's spicy fragrance and flavor are probably why it is considered an herb of the sun and fire, sacred to many of the sun gods. Magickally, it is used for healing, divination, love, protection, and it is said to raise spiritual vibrations in general. You can add cinnamon to your Midsummer foods or use it in incense. For something longer lasting, you can make this simple Summer Solstice cinnamon broom and use it to cast your ritual circle, decorate your Litha altar, or hang it up in your home to keep a little bit of summer's warmth around to lift your spirits in the darker months to come.

As with most craft projects, you can make this broom as simple or as fancy as you like, and add or change things to suit your tastes or the purpose for which you will use it. You will need:

- A small broom or whiskbroom (make sure you use one made of natural materials, not plastic). If you really want to get fancy, you can make your own broom from scratch.

- Newspapers

- A small paint brush

- White glue

- Powdered cinnamon

- A plastic or paper bag (large enough to fit the broom into)

- Ribbons in summer colors (yellow, orange, red, also possibly green and/or white) to decorate your broom with—the length you need will depend on the size of the broom you are using and how far you want them to hang; about a yard of each color should do

- Cinnamon essential oil (not fragrance oil, which is artificial) (optional)

- Dried summer flowers (roses, lavender, chamomile, daisies, sunflowers, asters, etc.) (optional)

- Cinnamon sticks or oak leaves or anything else you wish to add (optional)

- String or thread (you can use something fancy, like gold, or white is fine)

To make the basic cinnamon broom, place the broom on some newspapers or some other safe surface and use the brush to spread glue over one side of the broom. Sprinkle with cinnamon and place inside of bag overnight. If desired, you can repeat the next day with the other side.

Once you have your broom spiced up, you can add any decorations you want. Summer flowers can be hung from their stems (so that the flowers hang toward the bottom of the broom) and tied on with your thread or string. You can also hang additional cinnamon sticks or add a few drops of cinnamon essential oil for a stronger-smelling broom. If using oak leaves, glue or tie them on. Then tie the ribbons around the broom handle where it meets the broom itself, so they dangle down over the front of the broom.

If you want, you can set the broom out under the noon sun on Midsummer to catch the sun's energy and the blessings of the sun gods.

Gifts for the Birds

Midsummer is a celebration of the glories of the natural world, and the summer birds are part of that beauty and abundance. So why not share the party with our feathered friends by making up these simple treats that also do double duty as decorations for your yard. This is another fun one to do with kids.

You will need:

- Pinecones
- Apples
- Ribbons

- Peanut butter
- Birdseed
- Knitting needle or skewer to poke hole in apple (optional)

You can use either the pinecones or the apples as the base for your natural bird feeder, or both. If you are using the apples, you will want to poke a hole up through the middle using a knitting needle, skewer, or something like that. Start by tying a ribbon around the top of the pinecone or through the middle of the apple. Tie a large loop in the ribbon so you can hang it over a tree branch or hook.

Roll the pinecone or apple in peanut butter, and then roll in the birdseed until coated. (If you use the apple, the birds can eat that, too!) Then hang your decorative bird gifts where the birds can find and appreciate them.

Herb Crafting

Midsummer is also a time for herb craft of every kind. Herbs gathered on Midsummer are supposed to be at their most powerful, both for medicinal and magickal purposes. Here are some variations on traditional forms of herb crafting. Remember, just because something is natural doesn't mean it is safe. Be aware that some people are allergic to even the most common, mild herbs, such as lavender.

Herb craft doesn't have to be complicated. You can cut a sprig of rosemary and use it to sprinkle water during a ritual, or toss it on the bonfire for remembrance. Lavender is also thrown on the bonfire to honor the gods. Sage smudge sticks are wonderful for clearing away negative energy, and the scent of roses makes almost everyone think of love. For magickal crafts that are a little more involved, try one or two of these, either on

Midsummer itself, or in the days leading up to it, so you can have them ready to use on the day.

Love Sachet

This is a simple love sachet to draw love into your life. When you create it, you can concentrate on the kind of love you want, but try not to limit yourself to any one specific person or idea. After all, you never know what the universe might send if you leave the door open.

You will need:

- A square piece of cloth, about 3 inches by 3 inches, made out of some natural fabric (silk, cotton, etc.). Since this is a Midsummer sachet, you might want to use summer colors, instead of the usual pink.
- Either a ribbon to tie it with or a needle and thread
- Rose petals
- Lavender flowers
- A chunk of coal from a Midsummer bonfire, if you have one, to add extra power (optional)
- A small tumbled stone, such as rose quartz or amethyst or malachite (optional)

If possible, do this outside at noon on the Summer Solstice, when the heat of the sun can add to the power of the sachet. Otherwise, make it ahead of time and charge it under the sun.

Place your cloth on the grass or any flat surface, and place the flowers (and coal or stone if using) in the middle. If you are sewing it, then fold in half so you have three open sides and sew them shut starting at the bottom left and moving around to the right. Otherwise, gather the cloth together and tie it into a bundle with your ribbon.

Ask one of the love goddesses of Midsummer to bless it—Aphrodite, Venus, Astarte, Inanna, or Ishtar would all be good choices—and leave it out under the sun for a while if you can.

Sweet Dreams Pillow

Many cultures believed that if you used a particular charm on Midsummer Eve you would dream of love or your future husband. Various items were used, including oak flowers, mugwort, ash leaves, yarrow, and more. For this easy dream pillow, you will use a few of the herbs associated not only with divination and prophetic dreams, but with peaceful sleep as well. Hopefully, this will lead to sweet dreams. Maybe even dreams of true love.

You will need:

- A small drawstring bag or a square of cloth
- Needle and thread or a piece of ribbon

- Lavender flowers
- Calendula flowers (marigold)
- Chamomile flowers
- Rose petals (not necessarily used for sleep or dreaming, but they smell sweet, and will add the element of love to the pillow) (optional)

You can use either fresh or dried flowers for this. If you use fresh flowers, be aware that the moisture in the flowers will probably mean the pillow can only be used for a few nights before the flowers become vulnerable to mold. Dried flowers won't smell as nice, but they will last longer. If possible, pick the flowers yourself, out under the summer sun. If you can't, you may want to leave them on your altar, if you have one, for a night or two, or place them someplace where the sun will shine on them.

If using a drawstring bag, simply place all the items inside and close. If making a pillow, place the herbs in the middle of the cloth and either fold the cloth in half and sew from the bottom of one side, up and over and down the other, or tie it with the ribbon.

Hold the pillow in your hand before you go to sleep and think about what you wish to dream about, then tuck it under your pillow.

Wooden Wand

Midsummer is the perfect time to make yourself a simple magickal wand. You can use any of the types of wood associated with the Summer Solstice, such as oak, birch, hazel, or rowan. Apple, ash, elder, maple, and willow are also good. This is not the time to make a fancy or complicated wand—what you want is something that captures the elemental energy of the holiday. If possible, try to go out at or before dawn on the day of Midsummer.

Find a piece of wood, about the length of your forearm, or from the tip of your middle finger to your elbow. It should appeal to you both visually and spiritually, and feel *right* in your hand. You can use a piece that has already fallen from the tree. If you must cut a piece of wood off a living tree, ask the tree's permission, say thank you once you have done it, and bury a small gift at the foot of the tree.

If the piece of wood still has bark on it, you can either chose to leave it or peel it off with care and then polish lightly with sandpaper. The wood may be shaped with a knife or left as is. If you wish, you can carve or draw a few simple symbols onto the wood, such as a sun, a spiral, a snake, or some other sun or fire symbols.

Hazel Divining Rod

Midsummer is said to be one of the best times to collect hazel for use as a divining rod. It is sacred to the faeries and tied to the sun. Find a hazel tree or bush (there are many different species, but they will all work for this tool) and cut a forked piece with two prongs of equal length. There is no need to do anything else to it, unless you wish to bless it under the sun.

Divining rods are used by holding on to the two prongs, with the longer single piece held out in front of you. Hold the wood loosely, and walk slowly. The rod should dip to indicate the presence of water (or treasure, if you're lucky).

Decorating for the Solstice

Along with special foods and crafts that celebrate the holiday, another way to get into the mood is through decor. Whether this means adorning your home with holiday-themed decorations or setting up a special Midsummer altar, there are numerous options that fit in with the colors, symbols, and energies of the Summer Solstice. After all, most of us decorate the house for the Winter Solstice (Yule/Christmas), so why not do the same for its counterpart?

Whether you are adding to your regular altar or creating one specifically for Midsummer, here are some suggestions for things you may want to have on your Summer Solstice altar.

- Summer flowers, especially the rayed flowers that represent the sun, such as daisies, chamomile, marigold, asters, and sunflowers. These can be for decoration or as an offering to the goddess.

- Sun symbols—this also includes circles, spirals, disks, and wheels, as well as actual suns.

- The colors yellow, orange, red, and/or gold, as well as white or green. It is nice to have an altar cloth for the holiday that contains the sabbat colors, and if you use one it should definitely be "summery" feeling; bright and cheerful, perhaps with flowers on it.

- Incense that has a Midsummer-themed aroma, such as rose, lavender, cinnamon, lemon, or any of the others listed in the correspondences at the back of the book.

- A small cauldron to represent fire (you can put a candle in it, or just leave it empty).

- An "eternal flame" (in this case, a battery-powered light, since you won't want to leave a candle or actual flame burning when you are not present).

- Statues of any god or goddesses you worship at Midsummer.

- Fresh or dried oak leaves or acorns.

- Animal totems for the holiday, such as bees, butterflies, birds, etc.

- Gifts or offerings for the faeries.

- Gifts or offerings for the gods.

Anything else that seems appropriate to you. After all, it is your altar, and you should follow your heart when you decorate it. The same goes for decorating your home. If you are someone who goes all out, you may want to hang garlands of fresh flowers, change your regular tablecloth for one in a Midsummer color, put up a Midsummer-themed banner or flag (there are a number of these available online or at Pagan shops, and they can be quite beautiful), place bright yellow candles on various surfaces, and string up paper lanterns or flickering lights to represent the glow of the sun or the dance of fireflies.

If you are someone who prefers things more low-key, it may be enough to hang up a poster of Stonehenge or a carved wooden sun, and put a few extra items on the altar or mantelpiece. You may just pick some flowers and put them in the middle of the table. You may not decorate at all, choosing instead to simply go outside and enjoy the bright summer day. And that's fine too, since Midsummer is really about the glories of the natural world and the power of the sun overhead.

PRAYERS
AND
INVOCATIONS

beginnings, birth, renewal, rejuvenation, balance, fertility, chang

strength, vernal equinox, sun enters Aries, Libra in the Sou

Green Man, Amalthea, Aphrodite, Blodeuwedd, Eostre, Eo

, Flora, Freya, Gaia, Guinevere, Persephone, Libera, A

npet, Umaj, Vila, Aengus Mac Og, Cernunnos, Herma, The

Kama, Mabon Osiris, Pan, Thor, abundance, growth, health, ca

al healing, patience understanding virtue, spring, honor, contentu

hic abilities, spiritual truth, intuition, receptivity, love, inner se

provement, spiritual awareness, purification, childhood, innocence

ity, creativity, communication, concentration, divination, harmo

abilities, prosperity, attraction, blessings, happiness, luck, money,

y, guidance, visions, insight, family, wishes, celebrating life cy

iendship, courage, attracts love, honesty, good health, emotions,

improvement, influence, motivation, peace, rebirth, self preserva

ninine power, freedom, optimism, new beginnings, vernal equino

creation, sun, apple blossom, columbine, crocus, daffodil, daisy

sy, honeysuckle, jasmine, jonquil, lilac, narcissus, orange blosson

nrose, rose, the fool, the magician, the priestess, justice, the sta

s, gathering, growth, abundance, eggs, seeds, honey, dill, aspara

$\mathcal{W}$HETHER YOU ARE planning to celebrate the day with formal ritual or with simple, quiet, solitary practice (or both), it can be helpful to have a few invocations, meditations, affirmations, and prayers specifically designed for the sabbat. There are many ways to connect with the gods and with the energies of the season, and the following may be used on their own or as part of a larger ceremony.

Meditations are a way of letting go of the mundane world and moving the mind and spirit to another level. They should be done in as quiet and peaceful a space as possible, whether inside or outside. Make sure that you are in a comfortable position—some people like to lie down, others sit in a cross-legged, yoga-type seated position. Use whatever way is most comfortable for you and allows you to let go of focusing on your body and move inward instead.

There are a few different ways to do a meditation. Meditations can be read silently or aloud to yourself. Guided meditations are usually either done in a group setting, with one person (perhaps a priest or priestess, but not necessarily) reading aloud while everyone else listens with their eyes closed. If you want to do a guided meditation but have no one to read it, you can tape it ahead of time and then play it back for yourself.

To get the greatest benefit, you may want to start by closing your eyes and taking a few slow, deep breaths, consciously slowing down your breathing and your thoughts, so you are in a quieter mental and physical space to start from before the meditation begins.

Meditation on the Earth and Sun

This should be done sitting or standing on the ground, if possible.

Close your eyes. Take a deep, slow breath. Now another. Feel the strength of the earth underneath you. Solid and dependable, that strength is always there for you to call on if you need it. In your mind's eye, see yourself putting roots down into the ground, coming out of your tailbone or the soles of your feet, reaching deeper and deeper, down through the soil, deeper and deeper, toward the core of the earth itself. Feel your roots reaching down into the earth and connecting with that strength, that energy for growth. Feel that energy climbing up from the earth, up through those roots and into your own core, filling you with strength and calm and focus.

Now, reach upward and feel the power and the clarity that come from above. The vibrant energy from the sun, the clarity from the sky. Breathe it into the deepest core of your being. Feel the energy of the sun as it races through your veins and recharges your physical, mental, and spiritual batteries. Feel the light washing away all your stresses and cares, leaving only strength and clarity, calm and focus.

You are one with the earth. You are one with the sun. You are at peace. (Variation of Blake)

Meditation on Love

Love is one of the common themes of Midsummer. Love goddesses are revered, and it is not uncommon for handfastings and weddings to take place on this day. But love isn't limited to romantic love between two (or more) people. There is the love of family, and mother goddesses are also celebrated. Even those who are not fortunate enough to have a partner, or a family that they get along with, often have the love of friends, a coven, or a treasured furry companion. And not to forget, we have the love of the gods. This meditation focuses on opening ourselves to all the kinds of love there are.

If you want, before saying or listening to this mediation, you can light a pink or red candle and/or some rose or lavender incense and gather together pictures of those you love. If this is something you are really struggling with, you might also want to hold a crystal of rose quartz or amethyst during the meditation. Settle in a comfortable spot, surrounded by the candles and photographs. Read silently or aloud:

Like the rays of the sun on Midsummer,
love is everywhere.
Love is in the eyes of a mother as she looks at her child,
and so the goddess looks at us with eyes of love.
Love in the heart of our beloved, as it beats in unison
    with ours,
and so the goddess's heart beats with love for us.
Love is in the warmth of friendship that holds us close
    through the darkest hours,
and so the goddess is the light and the warmth,
    and she is love.
Love is the purr of the cat and the smooth fur of the dog, as
    they snuggle at our sides,
and so the goddess sends us those who will need us as we
    need them.
Love is the light and the path and the way,

and so we find love inside ourselves, for ourselves,
    and for others.
Love is all around us, like the rays of the sun above,
and so we open our hearts and our spirits to love
    and be loved.

Affirmations

Affirmations are short statements, usually said out loud, although they can be said silently to yourself. Always positive and always in the present tense ("I am loved and safe" not "I want to be loved and safe"), they help us to change the negative loops that repeat inside our brains and replace them with positive thoughts instead. It is believed (with some scientific indications that this belief is true) that by repeating positive affirmations, we can actually change our own personal reality. Affirmations are often done for healing, or for creating positive forward movements in our lives.

Try a few of these on the day of the Summer Solstice, and if they resonate with you, feel free to continue using them in the days that follow.

- I am as strong and vibrant as the summer sun. I am filled with energy.
- I am light and love, and I shine my light and love out into the world where it can be seen by others.

- I am beautiful, like the shining light of the sun.
- I am filled with light, moving in the direction I need to move in, following the path I am meant to walk.
- The God and Goddess love me, and so I blossom like the flowers.

God & Goddess Invocation

This is a good general invocation if you won't be working with any specific god or goddess. It can be used at the start of a ritual, or on its own.

Great goddess, I greet you! You who are known by many names and many faces, shine your divine blessing down on me on this Midsummer Day, filling me with light and love.

Great god, I greet you! You who are the lord of the beasts and the fields and the woods, shine your divine blessing down on me this Midsummer Day, filling me with strength and energy.

Invocation to Brighid and Belinos (Celtic)

This is a good invocation if you follow the Celtic pantheon. It can be used if you wish to ask for healing or inspiration.

I call thee, Brighid, triple goddess who rules over hearth and healing and inspiration. Share your gifts with me on this Summer Solstice day, and guide me with your gentle wisdom. Let your light warm my soul and brighten my spirit. So mote it be.

I call thee, Belinos, god of the sun, whose powerful rays bring healing and strength. Share your gifts with me on this Summer Solstice day, and empower me with your energy. Let your light warm my soul and brighten my spirit. So mote it be.

Invocation to Aphrodite and Apollo (Greek)

Use this invocation to the Greek god and goddess of light and love if you use the Greek pantheon. It can be used as a simple invocation for celebrating the aspects of the day.

Aphrodite! Blessed goddess of love, I invoke you and ask that you send me love in all its positive and life-affirming forms. Let this day be filled with love!

Apollo! Mighty god of the sun, I invoke you, as your chariot rolls across the sky bringing its life-giving rays. Let this day be filled with light and healing!

Invocation to Gaia

Gaia was originally a Greek earth and mother goddess, believed to have created the world. These days, she is often seen as a personification of the planet—the consciousness of the Earth itself. She is all that we worship, and all that we depend upon for sustenance. And she's getting the crap beaten out of her these days, what with one thing and another. Midsummer is a good time to invoke her, and thank her for all her gifts. It is always a good idea to be nice to your mother.

O Gaia, mother to us all, I invoke you!
You who gave birth to the world
have also given birth to me,
and I send you gratitude and love,
unending devotion, and the promise to guard over all
    your gifts.
Thank you for the mountains and the seas.
Thank you for the flowers and the trees and the crops in
    the field.
Thank you for the sun that shines and the rain that
    washes clean.
Thank you for our brothers the beasts, for the birds
    and the butterflies.
You are the beating heart of the earth,
strong beneath us, comforting around us.

You are our mother, and we are grateful.
You are our mother, and we love you.
Gaia! Gaia! Gaia!

Invocation to the Thunder Gods

Although the sun gods were the most worshipped on Litha, many cultures also paid homage to the gods of thunder, storms, and rain. If it is raining on Midsummer Day, or if you are living in a place that is suffering from the effects of drought, you may want to do an invocation to the thunder gods instead. If it is raining, you can copy the invocation and put it in a plastic bag to keep it dry, then say it standing out in the storm (as long as there is no lightning, of course). Some of these gods may be unfamiliar to you, and you might want to check the list of gods in the first chapter of this book to discover their origins and attributes. Perhaps one will inspire you to explore even further.

Gods of storm and gods of thunder!
Gods of lightning, powerful and bright!
Thank you for your life-bringing rains that fertilize the crops
    and the land.
Agni and Baal! Jupiter and Perun! I invoke you!
I call your healing waters and your storms, which wash clean.
Taranis and Thor! Thunar and Zeus! I invoke you!

I ask that your gifts be measured and steady.
That the rains come gently and the storms pass quickly,
harming none, and aiding all.
Bring your precious waters to the lands that have none
and ease your presence in the lands that have much.
Agni and Baal! Jupiter and Perun! I thank you!
Taranai and Thor! Thunar and Zeus! I thank you!
On this blessed Midsummer, I thank thee, and I praise
     thy names.

Invocation to Welcome the Dawn

If you are going to rise with the sun to greet the day on the
Summer Solstice, or if you are holding a vigil and staying up
until the dawn of the following day, you may want to use this
invocation to welcome the dawn. It can be said outside under
the brightening sky, or inside, at an altar or in front of an east-
facing window. Aurora is the Roman equivalent for the Greek
goddess of the dawn, Eos. This invocation should be said in a
soft voice, as befits the quiet morning calm.

Lovely Eos, goddess of the dawn, I welcome you.
Beautiful Aurora, goddess of the dawn, I welcome you.
As I look upon the beginning of a new day,
colored with your magickal palette of pinks and reds
     and oranges,

I marvel at the miracle that is the rising of the sun,
bringing with it light and warmth and possibilities as yet un-
known.
I welcome you, Eos, with love and gratitude for this new day.
I welcome you, Aurora, with love and gratitude for this new
day.
May it bring only happiness and joy to me and mine.
Welcome to the dawn of this new day.

Quarter Calls for Midsummer

These calls can be used to invoke the elements for a formal
ritual, or to cast a circle for solitary spellcasting. You can light
a candle as you say each quarter call, or simply turn to face the
direction associated with that quarter. Most people start with
the east/air, then turn to the south/fire, then west/water,
then north/earth. Some start with north instead.

East: I call the guardian of the east, the power of air, to
come to this circle bringing refreshing summer breezes
and lightness of spirit.

South: I call the guardian of the south, the power
of fire, to come to this circle bringing warm sunlight
and a passion for summer joy.

West: I call the guardian of the west, the power of water, to come to this circle bringing life-giving rains and flexible attitudes.

North: I call the guardian of the north, the power of earth, to come to this circle bringing energy for growth, and strength to rely on no matter what comes.

Prayer for Love

Prayers are a way of talking to the gods, and sending our wishes, desires, and pleas out into the universe. They can be very simple, and you don't need any special kind of ritual to say them. You may want to light a candle, if you are sitting or standing at your altar, or you can simply speak them from the heart.

Goddess, please send me love to fill my heart with joy and my days with warmth. Let me love and be loved in return, in the best way possible, for the good of all and according to the free will of all. And let that love be a reflection of your own great love, so that it might bring light into my life. So mote it be.

Prayer for Creativity

Brighid, let me bathe in your cauldron of creativity, and be touched by your gifts of inspiration and artistry. Let all I do be my very best, and help me to glow with the light of passionate creation, as bright as the Midsummer sun overhead.

Prayer for Healing

May the rays of the sun heal my body, mind, and spirit. May the warmth of this Midsummer Day chase away all illness and imbalance, and leave me healthy and whole. Gods of the sun, lend me your healing magick. Goddesses of the earth, lend me your healing magick. Let me be healthy and whole, my spirit glowing like the sun.

Prayer for Energy

May the power of the sun infuse me with positive energy. May the power of the vibrant and abundant earth fill me with vibrant and abundant positive energy. May the magick of Midsummer's Day bring me energy and purpose. So mote it be.

RITUALS
OF
CELEBRATION

beginnings, birth, renewal, rejuvenation, balance, fertility, change

strength, vernal equinox, sun enters Aries, Libra in the Zodi

Green Man, Amalthea, Aphrodite, Blodeuwedd, Eostre, Eo

Flora, Freya, Gaia, Guinevere, Persephone, Libera, Ma

pet, Umaj, Vila, Aengus MacOg, Cernunnos, Herma, The

ma, Mabon Osiris, Pan, Thor, abundance, growth, health, co

healing, patience understanding virtue, spring, honor, contentm

no abilities, spiritual truth, intuition, receptivity, love, inner sel

rovement, spiritual awareness, purification, childhood, innocence,

ty, creativity, communication, concentration, divination, harmon

bilities, prosperity, attraction, blessings, happiness, luck, money,

guidance, visions, insight, family, wishes, celebrating life cyc

ndship, courage, attracts love, honesty, good health, emotions,

improvement, influence, motivation, peace, rebirth, self preservat

mine power, freedom, optimism, new beginnings, vernal equinox

reation, sun, apple blossom, columbine, crocus, daffodil, daisy,

y, honeysuckle, jasmine, jonquil, lilac, narcissus, orange blossom,

rose, rose, the fool, the magician, the priestess, justice, the star

gathering, growth, abbundance, eggs, seeds, honey, dill, aspara

$\mathcal{T}$HERE ARE MANY different ways to celebrate the sabbats. Some people simply use the holidays as occasions for merriment and feasting, gathering with witchy friends to enjoy the day in an informal fashion. On Midsummer, that usually means picnics, barbecues, camping, or a day out at the beach. Others observe the sabbats with rituals—some as solitaries on their own; others with a coven or with a group of folks who otherwise practice by themselves but like to get together for holidays; or even at a large gathering, if there happens to be such a thing near where they live. There are also people who hold small rituals for their family, sharing their faith with their children as many have throughout the ages.

Some people like to write their own rituals, while others are more comfortable using rites that someone else has devised. Here are three examples of rituals that you can use as is, or adapt as desired to fit your own needs. Keep in mind that you can take elements of the solitary ritual and create a group or family ritual out of them, and that the third ritual—in theory designed for families or children—is perfectly appropriate for fun-loving adults, whether individuals or groups.

You can also take elements from the previous chapter on spells and divination, and use those as the core of a Midsummer ritual, shaping them as desired and then using the ritual basics (quarter calls, god and goddess invocations and dismissals, etc.) listed here for the rest of the ritual. Or even use one or more of the crafts listed in the chapter on recipes and crafts to create a fun and entertaining "crafty" ritual.

It is also possible to make even mundane activities like picnics or barbecues into rituals, if you hold them in sacred space and invite the gods to join you. Or you can incorporate some of the old traditions (as listed in Chapter One) into a modern form that suits your own practice, thus creating your own new traditions, for yourself or for those you share your practice with on this, the day of the Summer Solstice.

The Solitary Midsummer: Drawing Down the Sun

In Wiccan magickal workings, there is a practice known as "Drawing Down the Moon," in which a witch (usually, but not always, a priestess) channels the Goddess by drawing Her essence into herself. Less common is the practice of "Drawing Down the Sun," in which a (usually male) witch channels the God. This is not that kind of drawing down the sun.

Purpose:

This ritual's focus is on pulling in the power of the sun at its zenith and taking that energy inside yourself, where it will charge your own spiritual battery in preparation for the darker months to come. The ritual is fairly simple, with few tools needed, and it is perfect for both the experienced practitioner and one who is new to the path. It can also be converted relatively easily to a group ritual, if desired.

Setting:

This should be done at noon if possible, on the day of Midsummer. If necessary, it can be done at any point during the day as long as the sun is still shining overhead. If it is raining on the actual day, the energy will still be much the same within a couple of days before and after, although not quite as powerful. As with most other Midsummer rituals, this one is best done outside, under the sun, preferably in the middle of an open area like a meadow or a yard. It can also be done on a beach or anyplace where you will be sitting where the sun is shining on you. If you can't be outside, try to find a spot inside where the sun will fall directly on you while you are doing the ritual, even if that means performing it before or after noon in order to have the sun shining in the right place.

Supplies:

You need god and goddess candles (gold/silver or yellow/white or white/white) in fire-safe holders, four quarter candles (one each green/yellow/red/blue), a pillar candle to represent the sun (yellow or orange or red). You also need a cast iron cauldron or fire-safe container or candle holder, salt and water in small containers, a small bowl to mix them in, incense or a sage smudge stick in a holder or bowl, wide ribbon in a color that matches your sun candle (if your candle is yellow, use a yellow ribbon, etc.) long enough to tie around your waist, matches, sun-shaped or round cookies for cakes and ale (you can make sugar cookies and coat them with yellow frosting if you want), fruit juice or wine or mead or ale in a chalice or fancy cup. Optional—sunflowers or daisies as an offering for the gods, candle snuffer, athame, broom, or wand, decorative altar cloth, table to use as an altar, blanket or cloth to sit on if you are going to be outside.

Notes: While the instructions call for a full ritual set-up, if you don't have everything listed here, don't worry. The tools are meant to help you focus, and to heighten the sense of ceremony, and they will probably make your ritual even more powerful. But if you are not in a position to do the entire formal ritual (for instance, if you are not out of the broom closet, and you need something you can do quickly and without being obvious about it), you can do the core section of the ritual on its own.

Pre-Ritual Preparations:

Place the god and goddess candles on your altar or in the middle of your circle (depending on whether you are using a formal altar or simply placing things on the ground or floor). Put the pillar candle in its holder between them, toward the front of the space, so you can sit in front of it easily, and tie the ribbon in a loose circle around the base of the holder. Place any offerings or decorations on the altar. Quarter candles can be placed on the altar in their proper directions, or at the edges of the circle, with the candle for earth facing north, air facing east, fire to the south, and water to the west. Cakes and ale can be placed to the side, where you can reach them when the ritual is nearing its end.

The Ritual:

Start by cleansing the space and yourself by smudging it with the sage wand (or incense). Walk around the circle clockwise, moving the smoke through the air, and visualizing your ritual area being washed clear of any negativity. Then do the same thing with yourself, starting at your head and working down to your feet. You can leave the sage/incense smoldering in its holder or put it out.

Pour a little bit of salt into the small bowl, and add a little water. As you mix them together with your finger or an athame, say:

Salt into water, water into salt. Wash away all that is negative and impure, leaving only that which is positive and beneficial.

Dab the salt and water mixture on your forehead (for thoughts), lips (for speech), and heart (for feelings).

Cast the circle by walking its parameters and pointing toward the ground (you can use your finger, an athame, a broom, or a wand—if using a broom, make sweeping motions but keep the broom slightly above the surface of the ground), saying:

Earth to sky, sky to ground; let sacred space be all around.

Visualize your circle filling with white light, enclosing you in a space that is outside of normal time or place.

Call the quarters, starting with the east. Turn to the east and say:

I call the guardian of the east, the power of air,
to come to this circle bringing refreshing summer breezes
and lightness of spirit.

Light the yellow candle. Turn to the south and say:

I call the guardian of the south, the power of fire,
to come to this circle bringing warm sunlight
and a passion for summer joy.

Light the red candle. Turn to the west and say:

I call the guardian of the west, the power of water,
to come to this circle bringing life-giving rains and a healing flow.

Light the blue candle. Turn to the north and say:

I call the guardian of the north, the power of earth,
to come to this circle bringing energy for growth
and the strength of the ground below.

Light the green candle. Then, invoke the gods, using the words here or any of the alternatives in the previous chapter.

Great goddess, I greet you! You who are known by many names
and many faces, shine your divine blessing down on me on
this Midsummer Day, filling me with light and love.

Great god, I greet you! You who are the lord of the beasts and the
fields and the woods, shine your divine blessing down on me this
Midsummer Day, filling me with strength and energy.

Light the god and goddess candles.

Stand (or sit, if necessary) in front of your altar and light the candle that represents the sun. Close your eyes and lift your arms up into the air, as if reaching for the sun overhead, palms open and turned up. Feel the warmth of the sun on your face; feel its life-giving energy flowing into you through the crown chakra on the top of your head and down to fill your entire body. See yourself glowing with light and energy. Keep this image in your mind as strongly as you can, taking as long as you need. Then open your eyes and look at the candle. The flame in the candle symbolizes the heat and power of the sun—see that energy moving also into the candle, and from the candle, into the ribbon that is underneath it. Say:

Today is Midsummer and the sun is at its zenith. Its power and
energy are all around me. Its power and energy are part of me.
I am the fire of the sun.

Pick up the ribbon, hold it up to the sun, and then tie it around your waist. Feel the strength of the sun inside the ribbon, and say:

Within this token, I store the power and energy of the sun,
that they may carry me through the darker days ahead.

Cakes and ale (optional): Hold up your "cake" and say,

I thank the earth for its harvest
and for the bounty it brings to my life.

Eat the cake. Hold up your cup and say,

I thank the sun for its life-giving rays that help the harvest to grow
and bring sweetness to this cup and to my life.

Drink the ale. Thank the god and goddess by saying:

Blessed lady, blessed lord, I thank you for your presence
in my circle here today and in my life always.

Snuff out the god and goddess candles.

Now it is time to dismiss the quarters. Starting at the north and turning counterclockwise (west, south, east), say in each direction:

I thank you (insert name of element in the order of: earth, water,
fire, air) for watching over my circle and my magickal work.

Snuff out the candles after thanking each element.

Open the circle by turning counterclockwise and pointing as you turn. Visualize a wall of light dropping down until you are back into your normal life. Take a moment to let it all sink in. You can wear your ribbon all day, or take it off and put it away someplace safe like a box or a bag that can be stored on your altar or in a special drawer. Anytime you feel as though you need an extra boost, you can take it out and either wear it (under your clothes if you choose) or put it in a pocket.

Midsummer Healing and Abundance Group Ritual

Midsummer is the perfect time for magickal healing work, as well as work for abundance. This ritual combines them both by using the healing energy of the sun and the fire that is its symbol. The fire will burn away those things that hold you back, so you can then take in the energy for abundance and growth that is the hallmark of this sabbat. This ritual is designed for a group, whether it is a formal coven or simply a gathering of like-minded witches, but you can convert it for solitary use if necessary.

If your group follows a specific pantheon, feel free to substitute a different god and goddess. This ritual is intended to be done around a bonfire or fire pit (you can use a portable fire pit rather than digging one in the ground). If you can't be outside or can't have an open fire, you can substitute a firesafe cauldron or other large round container, and fill it with sand or salt, and then place candles inside to take the place of the fire. As always, please be cautious when using any kind of open flame, especially if wearing flowing garb. Always have a bucket of water or some other way of smothering the fire nearby in case it suddenly gets out of hand. Group rituals are almost always led by a high priest and/or a high priestess, or someone who is taking those roles for the occasion. This ritual is written for one leader, but it can be split between two if you wish, or divided between all the participants, so that each one speaks a different section of the ritual.

Setting:

This ritual can be done at any point on Midsummer Day, although the most powerful time will be dusk, just as the sun is getting ready to go down. Leave enough time to complete the ritual before the sun vanishes entirely, though. It should be held outside, if possible, preferably around a bonfire.

Supplies:

You will need god and goddess candles (gold/silver or yellow/white or white/white) in fire-safe holders. You will also need four quarter candles (one each green/yellow/red/blue). Gather salt and water in small containers, a small bowl to mix them in, a sage smudge stick (you can substitute a stick of incense if you prefer) in a fire safe container, lavender flowers in a basket or bowl, daisies or some other bright flower (one for each participant) in a basket, matches, food and drink for cakes and ale (either a round loaf of bread or some cheerful cookies for cakes, and fruit juice, wine, or mead for ale in a chalice or other nice cup), table to use as an altar. If you like, you can also use a candlesnuffer, a cauldron or a bowl with candles in it if you can't have a bonfire, cloth for the altar, a feather, and any other seasonal decorations, such as a vase of flowers or sun symbols.

Pre-Ritual Preparations:

Place god and goddess candles on your altar with your baskets of lavender and flowers or herbs nearby. Place any offerings or decorations on the altar. Quarter candles can be placed on the altar in their proper directions, or at the edges of the circle, with the green candle for earth facing north, the yellow air candle facing east, the red fire candle to the south, and the blue water candle to the west. Cakes and ale can be placed to the side, where you can reach them when the ritual is nearing its end. The altar can be placed wherever it fits best in the circle, or you can put it in the east, since that is the direction associated with fire, and therefore the sun. The bonfire should be lit before you start.

The Ritual:

Start by cleansing the space and all the participants by smudging it with the sage wand (or incense). Someone should walk around the circle clockwise, moving the smoke through the air, and visualizing the ritual area being washed clear of any negativity. A feather can be used to waft the smoke inward if desired. Then pass the sage around the circle clockwise so each participant can sage him or herself, starting at the head and working down to the feet. Once the sage/incense returns to the beginning, it can be left smoldering in its holder or put out.

The leader should pour a little bit of salt into the small bowl, and add a little water, mixing them together with a finger or an athame, saying:

Salt into water, water into salt.
Wash away all that is negative and impure,
leaving only that which is positive and beneficial.

Pass the bowl around the circle. Each participant then dabs the salt and water mixture on his/her forehead (for thoughts), lips (for speech), and heart (for feelings).

The leader will cast the circle by walking the circle parameters pointing toward the ground. He/she can use a finger, an athame, a broom, or a wand—if using a broom, make sweeping motions, but keep the broom slightly above the surface of the ground. As he/she walks the circle, say:

> *I cast the circle round and round, from earth to sky,*
> *from sky to ground. I conjure now this sacred place,*
> *outside of time, outside of space. The circle is cast.*
> *We are between the worlds.*

Next the group will call the quarters. This can be done by the leader or four participants can each take a turn. All in the circle will turn in the direction of the quarter being called, the invocation is spoken, and the associated candle is lit. Then, all turn toward the next quarter. Start with east by saying:

> *I call the guardian of the east, the power of air,*
> *to come to this circle bringing refreshing summer breezes*
> *and clarity of thought.*

Light the yellow candle. Turn to the south and say:

> *I call the guardian of the south, the power of fire,*
> *to come to this circle bringing warm sunlight and the spirit of love.*

Light the red candle. Turn to the west and say:

I call the guardian of the west, the power of water,
to come to this circle bringing life-giving rains and healing energy.

Light the blue candle. Turn to the north and say:

I call the guardian of the north, the power of earth,
to come to this circle and ground us for the magickal work ahead.

Light the green candle.
The leader should now invoke the gods using the words here or any of the alternatives in the previous chapter by saying:

I call thee, Brighid, triple goddess who rules over hearth and healing
and inspiration. Share your gifts with us on this Summer Solstice
day, and guide us with your gentle wisdom.
Let your light warm our hearts and brighten our spirits.
So mote it be.

Light the goddess candle.

I call thee, Belinos, god of the sun,
whose powerful rays bring healing and strength.
Share your gifts with us on this Summer Solstice day,
and empower us with your energy. Let your light warm our hearts
and brighten our spirits. So mote it be.

Light the god candle. Then the ritual leader should say:

We gather together to celebrate Midsummer, the Summer
Solstice. This is the longest day of the year, with the most
light, and the sun is at the height of its power and energy.
After today, we move slowly into the dark time, with a little
less light and a little more darkness every day. So it always
has been, and so it will always be, for this is the Wheel
of the Year, always turning, bringing us opportunities for
change and growth.

The sun god is a healing god, and the earth goddess heals
as well. Today we will tap into that healing power and use it
to help us to let go of whatever ails us—physically, mentally,
or spiritually—so that we will be free to take in the sun's
energy, and use it to bring abundance into our lives.

The leader holds up bowl of lavender and says:

Lavender is one of the most healing herbs there is, sacred
to the Midsummer gods. In some cultures, it is customary
to throw lavender into the fire as an offering to the god and
goddess. As we go around the circle, each one of us will take
a turn to toss in a handful of these fragrant flowers, casting
whatever needs to be healed into the cleansing flames of the
fire as we do so.

The bowl is passed around, and each participant tosses in some lavender. If doing this without an actual bonfire, you can either sprinkle a tiny amount of lavender carefully around the candles in their bowl, or place a plate underneath the central candles and put the lavender on that. Once everyone has sprinkled lavender, the leader says:

Now we are free to receive the solstice's blessings of energy, abundance, and joy! Take a flower as a symbol of the abundant Midsummer energy, and feel your spirit filling up with potential as I lead us in a guided meditation.

Pass the basket of flowers around the circle. Each participant will take one. All stand in silence and focus on taking in energy as they listen. The leader continues with:

Close your eyes if you want to, or focus them on the flower in your hands. The summer days are filled with light and beauty, and we can take in that light, take in that beauty, and make it a part of ourselves. Feel the warmth of the sun overhead. The sun's power is at its peak, and there is more than enough to share with us. Feel the energy of the sun coming in at the top of your head and flowing down through you—over your head, neck, and shoulders. Feel it flowing down over your arms like a caress, down your back like a gentle massage. Feel the power and energy of the sun recharging your own center of energy in your core, filling it with everything you need to live each day of the summer to its fullest. Let it flow down your legs, through your fingers and toes, making them tingle with warmth and light and power. Imagine your body filled with that light so that it spills out into the circle around you, and see the entire circle glowing with light and energy, moving from person to person, picking up love and joy on its journey and passing it around until everyone within this sacred space is filled to overflowing with the power and energy and glory that is the summer sun. Hold your flower to your heart, and then raise it to the sun with a heartfelt "Thank you and huzzah!"

All shout: *Thank you and huzzah!*

The leader holds up the plate with cakes and says:

> *We give thanks for these cakes, the gift of the earth,*
> *and share them with each other with open hearts.*

The cakes are passed around the circle. The leader holds up the chalice or cup and says:

> *May our lives be as sweet as the fruit in this cup.*

The cup is passed around circle. The leader then thanks the gods by saying:

Let us thank the god and goddess
for their gifts of healing and energy!

All shout: *Thank you, Belinos! Thank you, Brighid!* This can be repeated a number of times, all participants following the leader. When done, snuff out the god and goddess candles.

Next, the leader dismisses the quarters. This is done in the reverse of how the quarters were called, starting with north, then turning counterclockwise to west, south, and finally east. The leader or participants say for each quarter:

I thank you (insert name of element in order of: earth, water,
fire, air) for guarding our circle. Stay if you will, go if you must,
in perfect love and perfect trust. So mote it be.

Snuff out the candles after thanking each element.

Once the quarters are dismissed, open the circle. The leader can walk counterclockwise and draw the energy back in, or all can join hands and throw them up into the sky, saying:

The circle is open but never broken. Merry meet, merry part,
and merry meet again!

A Small Group Ritual for Playing with the Faeries

This is a fun, playful ritual, perfect for doing with small children. It can also be done by a couple, or with any small group. If you are doing it with young children, keep things as simple as possible, and let them be a part of the ritual. Feel free to be informal and silly!

The faeries should always be treated with respect, but they are also known for their mischievous nature. If you do this ritual just right, perhaps they will come and play along with you. Even if you don't sense any mystical presences, it is nice to take some time to focus on the lighthearted aspects of Midsummer. If you are doing this ritual with children, depending on their ages and level of experience with magickal work (some people raise their children as Pagan from a very early age and others don't), you may want to skip the formal circle casting. If so, you will still want to do some protective work first, just to be on the safe side. For instance, you could smudge the area where you will be working and draw a circle in salt or chalk. This ritual is designed to have one person lead it, but the tasks can be shared by two or more if you wish.

Setting:

This ritual should be done at noon, dawn, or dusk as the faeries are most likely to come out at one of these "between" times. But anytime on Midsummer Day is fine, or even on

Midsummer Eve. It should be done outside, in a space with greenery and flowers. If there are no flowers, you can provide your own, but this ritual really should be done outdoors. Although if you are doing it with kids, their imaginations are so wonderful, you can probably create a make-believe faery grove inside, if you absolutely have to.

Supplies:

You will need god and goddess candles (gold/silver or yellow/white or white/white) in fire-safe holders. You will also need four quarter candles (one each green/yellow/red/blue), a sage smudge stick (you can substitute a stick of incense if you prefer), bottles of bubbles, matches, food and drink for cakes and ale (some cheerful cookies for cakes, and fruit juice for ale, unless there are only adults, in which case mead is appropriate). You should have a table to use as an altar, plus a small table or a cloth to put in the middle of the circle to receive the gifts for the faeries. Provide music to dance to as well. If you like, you can also gather a candlesnuffer, cloth for the altar, and any other seasonal decorations.

You will also need gifts for the faeries—enough for each person to give one. These can be natural objects like pretty little stones, a small bowl of honey, rose petals in a bowl, or some flowers such as daisies, marigolds, or carnations. But you may also opt to throw in a craft project and make fun paper flowers or glittery stars. These can be made ahead of time or during the ritual (instructions below) for kids with longer attention spans. If you opt to do this, you'll need the following supplies: tissue paper and/or colored paper in bright flowery colors, pipe cleaners, scissors, tape or thread, white glue, a small brush, glitter or glitter glue. Place all of the supplies on a cloth or do this outside, since it will be a little messy (especially the glitter). If making this craft during ritual, have all supplies within the circle ahead of time.

Pre-Ritual Preparations:

Place the god and goddess candles on the altar table along with any other decorations. If there is room on the table, you can put all the other supplies there too, otherwise you can stow some underneath where you can get at them easily. The quarter candles can be placed around the circle in their proper spots (yellow air candle to the east, red fire candle to the south, blue water candle to the west, and green earth candle to the north) unless you are worried about small children getting at them, in which case you can either put them on the altar table or dispense with their use altogether. Make sure that every participant has a bottle of bubbles. If there are kids who are young enough to want to get into the bubbles before you are ready, you can hand them out when it is time. The table or cloth for the faerie gifts should go as close to the middle of the circle as possible.

The Ritual:

Start by cleansing the space and all the participants by smudging it with the sage wand (or incense). Someone should walk around the circle clockwise, moving the smoke through the air, and visualizing the ritual area being washed clear of any negativity. Then pass the sage around the circle clockwise so each participant can sage him or herself, starting at the head and working down to the feet. Or one person can walk around the outside of the circle and smudge all those within, if there are kids too young to handle the sage themselves.

Feel free to skip this circle casting section if you have small children or wish to do something more casual. To cast the circle, take a flower from the altar and pass it from person to person, starting with whoever is leading the ritual, saying:

With this flower, we cast the circle.

Next, call the quarters. If possible, have the kids help call the quarters. If they are very young, they can simply call, "East, east, please come here!" Turn in the direction of the quarter you are calling, starting with east, and say:

I call the guardian of the east, the power of air,
upon which the faeries fly.

Light the yellow candle. Then turn to the south and say:

I call the guardian of the south, the power of fire,
which lights the faeries' way.

Light the red candle. Turn to the west and say:

I call the guardian of the west, the power of water,
like the magickal Midsummer dew where the fairies like to bathe.

Light the blue candle, then turn to the north and say:

I call the guardian of the north, the power of earth,
where the faeries love to play.

Light the green candle. Next, the leader should invoke the gods using the words here or any of the alternatives in the previous chapter by saying:

Lovely Aine, goddess of the faeries, come and join our circle today!

Light the goddess candle. Then say:

Handsome Belinos, who causes the flowers to grow,
come and join our circle today!

Light the god candle. The leader then says:

Today is Midsummer, the day the faeries come out to play.
Shall we welcome them? HAIL FAERIES, AND WELCOME!

All repeat, loudly and with enthusiasm. If you have brought gifts to the circle, continue with:

We have brought you gifts, O faerie folk, in the hopes that you will
smile upon us and send us your blessings.

Each person walks up to the altar and takes a "gift" and puts in on the table / cloth in the middle of the circle, saying:

Here is a gift for you, faeries!

If you instead are opting to incorporate a fun craft into the ritual, then say:

We are making you gifts, O faerie folk, in the hopes that you will
smile upon us and send us your blessings.

Proceed to where you've stashed your craft supplies. To create pretty flowers for the faeries, you can form the tissue paper into a flower by cutting it into square pieces and then crimping the bottom closed with one hand while spreading out the "petals" with another. To make a fancier flower, layer a couple of different colors, or cut the edges into particular flower shapes. Then, tie a bit of thread around the bottom third of the flower to keep its form. Use a pipe cleaner for the stem by poking it up through the very bottom of the flower and securing it with glue or tape.

Alternately, you can cut flower shapes out of your colored paper and tape or glue a stem onto the bottom. Use the brush to put a light coating of glue around the top edges or outside of the flower and sprinkle with glitter. If using glitter glue sticks, apply where desired. Add any other decorations if using. Once the glue has dried, put the flowers on your altar or outside for the faeries.

Using the same supplies, you could make an alternate craft. Cut out stars from brightly colored construction paper and decorate with glitter, bells, markers, etc. Then, punch a hole in each one and string them up on thread or ribbons to make a garland to adorn your faery altar and give as a gift to the fair folk. Hang up finished strands where the sun can catch the glitter and make it shine.

Whether made ahead of time or during the ritual itself, when all the gifts are in the middle of the circle, the leader can say things like:

Oh, how beautiful those gifts are!
I'm sure the faerie folk will love them!

Then, pass out the bubbles if you haven't done it already. When everyone has bubbles, the leader says:

We can make magick, too, with water and light and air!
Come join us, faeries, and let us dance together!

All blow bubbles and dance around the circle with as much merriment as possible. When you are done, everyone says:

Thank you, faeries, for joining us today!
Huzzah for the faeries of Midsummer Day!

Next, pass cakes and ale if you are having them, making sure to put a little bit aside for the faeries. If you want, the leader can say:

Faerie folk, please join us for some treats.
Thank you lord and lady for your presence here today.
Thank you lord and lady for helping us to play.

Snuff out the god and goddess candles. Next, dismiss the quarters by having everyone say:

> *Thank you, north! Thank you, west! Thank you, south!*
> *Thank you, east! Goodbye! Goodbye!*

Snuff out the quarter candles. Once the quarters are dismissed, open the circle if you cast one by having the leader say:

> *The circle is open, but never broken. Merry meet, merry part,*
> *and merry meet again!*

Or, if there are very young children, you can just say:

> *We're done! That was fun!*

CORRESPONDENCES
FOR
MIDSUMMER

beginnings, birth, renewal, rejuvenation, balance, fertility, change

strength, vernal equinox, sun enters Aries, Libra in the Sou

Green Man, Amalthea, Aphrodite, Blodeuwedd, Eostre, Eo

Flora, Freya, Gaia, Guinevere, Persephone, Libera, M

pet, Umaj, Vila, Aengus MacOg, Cernunnos, Herma, The

ama, Mabon Osiris, Pan, Thor, abundance, growth, health, ca

healing, patience understanding virtue, spring, honor, contentm

hic abilities, spiritual truth, intuition, receptivity, love, inner sel

rovement, spiritual awareness, purification, childhood, innocence,

ty, creativity, communication, concentration, divination, harmo

bilities, prosperity, attraction, blessings, happiness, luck, money,

guidance, visions, insight, family, wishes, celebrating life cyc

ndship, courage, attracts love, honesty, good health, emotions,

improvement, influence, motivation, peace, rebirth, self preserva

mine power, freedom, optimism, new beginnings, vernal equinox

reation, sun, apple blossom, columbine, crocus, daffodil, daisy,

y, honeysuckle, jasmine, jonquil, lilac, narcissus, orange blossom,

rose, rose, the fool, the magician, the priestess, justice, the star

gathering, growth, abundance, eggs, seeds, honey, dill, aspara

Spiritual Focus and Key Words

Abundance

cleansing

creativity

divination

fertility

fire

growth

healing

inspiration

love

motherhood

opportunity

power

success

sun god energy

warmth

Magickal Focus

Abundance

empowerment

energy

fertility

growth

health

increase

light (longest day of the year)

love

motherhood

Suggested Workings

Bidding farewell to the waxing half of the year

celebrating the sun

connecting with the earth and/or growing things

green magick

harvesting herbs (especially healing herbs)

honoring the pregnant goddess/the god at his peak

weddings and handfastings

working with the faeries

Astrological Timing and Associated Planets

Summer solstice is the longest day of the year, no matter which hemisphere you are in. It begins when the sun enters Cancer (in the Northern Hemisphere) or Capricorn (in the Southern Hemisphere), usually around June 21 in the North (varying from June 20 to 22) or December 21 in the South (varying from December 20 to 23).

Archetypes

FEMALE

Earth Mother

the Fairy Queen

Goddess in the form of the Mother

Goddess of fertility and pregnant goddesses

love goddesses

sun goddesses

MALE

the Fairy King

Fire gods

"leafy" gods, such as Green George, Jack O' the Green, the Green Man, the Holly King, the Oak King, or Pan

the Seven-Year King (Celtic gods who ruled for seven years and then were sacrificed for the good of the people and the land)

sun gods

thunder gods

Deities and Heroes

GODDESSES

Aestas (Roman)

Aine (Celtic)

Amaterasu (Japanese)

Amaunet (Egyptian)

Anuket (Egyptian)

Aphrodite (Greek)

Arani (Hindu)

Artemis (Greek)

Astarte (Canaanite)

Athena (Greek)

Aurora (Roman)

Bast (Egyptian)

Bona Dea (Roman)

Brighid/Brigit (Celtic)

Cerridwin (Welsh)

Eos (Greek)

Epona (Celtic)

Frigga (Teutonic)

Gaia (Greek)

Hathor (Egyptian)

Hera (Greek)

Hestia (Greek)

Iarila (Russian)

Inanna (Sumerian)

Ishtar (Assyrian)

Juno (Roman)

Rhiannon (Welsh)

Saule (Baltic)

Sekhmet (Egyptian)

Solntse (Russian)

Sul (Celtic)

Sunna (German)

Vesta (Roman)

Yemaya (African)

GODS

Agni (Hindu)

Amun-Ra (Egyptian)

Apollo (Greek/Roman)

Baal (Phoenician)

Balder/Baldur (Scandinavian)

Belinos (Celtic)

Bochica (South African)

Hadad (Babylonian)

Helios (Greek)

Hoder/Hodur (Norse)

Hu (Celtic)

Huitzilopochtli (Aztec)

Hyperion (Greek)

Janus (Roman)

Jupiter (Roman)

Kupalo (Slavic/Russian)

Lleu Llaw Gyffes (Welsh)

Llew (Welsh)

Lugh (Irish)

Marduk (Assyrian)

Maui (Polynesian)

Mithras (Persian)

Odin (Norse)

Orunjan (Yoruban)

Perun (Hindu)

Prometheus (Greek)

Ra (Egyptian)

Shamash (Assyro-Babylon)

Sol (Roman)

Taranis (British)

Thor (Norse)

Thunar (Anglo-Saxon)

Vishnu (Vedic)

Woden (Anglo-Saxon)

Xiuhtecuti (Aztec)

Zeus (Greek)

Colors

Gold: Energy, power, prosperity, solar deities, strength, success, the God, the sun, wisdom

Green: Abundance, calming, fertility, growth, new beginnings, prosperity

Orange: Adaptability, communication, courage, creativity, energy, optimism, success

Red: Anger, courage, creativity, desire, energy, fire, lust, passion, sexual love, strength, willpower

White: Cleansing, divination, healing, innocence, peace, protection, purification, truth

Yellow: Communication, creativity, dream work, happiness, intelligence, learning, protection, psychic ability, the sun, willpower

Herbs

Cinnamon: Energy, love, power, prosperity, psychic ability

Foxglove: Faery energy, healing, protection

Mistletoe: Fertility, healing, love, protection, strength

Mugwort: Clairvoyance, divination, dreams, psychic ability

Rosemary: Love, memory, protection, purification, wisdom

St. John's Wort: Happiness, healing, protection, strength

Vervain: Healing, magick, power, protection, purification

Yarrow: Healing, love, marriage protection, psychic ability

Trees

Elder: Blessings, faeries, healing
Hazel: Fertility, luck, protection
Oak: Life, protection, strength
Rowan: Clairvoyance, divination, protection

Flowers

Chamomile: Calming, communication, determination,
   harmony, intuition, prosperity, purification
Daisy: Love, luck, omens
Heather: Awareness, generosity, growth, protection
Lavender: Healing, love, peace, purification, sleep
Marigold: Healing, peace, protection
Meadowsweet: Harmony, love, peace
Rose: Attraction, love, peace, protection, sex

Crystals and Stones

Carnelian: Courage, healing, peace, protection, sexual energy
Citrine: Abundance, balance, protection, psychic awareness
Diamond: Courage, healing, protection, spirituality, strength
Emerald: Love, memory, protection, psychic powers
Jade: Healing, longevity, love, prosperity, protection, wisdom
Peridot: Prosperity, protection
Tiger-eye: Courage, energy, luck, prosperity

Metals

Copper: Energy, love, luck, healing, prosperity, protection

Gold: Prosperity, protection, success, wisdom

Animals, Totems, and Mythical Creatures

Bees: Abundance, messengers from the spirits, new life, sweetness (because of the honey they make)

Bull: Fertility, power, strength (associated with the God and kingship)

Butterflies: Rebirth (they change from inert chrysalis to beautiful flying creature), the soul

Cow: Abundance, mother goddesses (because of the milk cows give), wealth

Hawks and eagles: Seen as solar birds because they soared so high, also power and strength

Horse: Power, sex, strength, swiftness

Swallows, wrens, and other summer birds: Rebirth, renewal, warmth

Scents for Oils, Incense, Potpourri, or Just Floating in the Air

Cinnamon

heliotrope

lavender

lemon

newly mown grass

orange

peppermint

pine

rose

sandalwood

spearmint

the scent of flowers

Tarot keys

The Empress

the Emperor

the Sun

Strength

Symbols and Tools

Balefire or bonfire (fire): Goodwill, purification

Cauldron: Abundance, divine inspiration

Faeries (the magickal world): Creativity, life, transformation

Rosettes and Roses: Fire, sun goddesses

Sacred Wells: The Goddess, water

Solar Cross/Sun Wheel: Symbol of the movement of the sun marked by the soltices

Spinning Wheels: The Goddess is sometimes thought to have spun the world and the rays of the sun on her spinning wheel

Spirals: Symbol of the sun's path through the year

Wand: Power, strength, will

Foods

Berries

cheese

cinnamon toast (or any other food made with cinnamon)

grapes

honey

lemons

oranges

peaches

pears

pine nuts

pumpernickel bread

spinach

summer squash

sunflower seeds

sun-dried tomatoes

Drinks

Ale

lemonade

mead

milk (for the faeries)

mint tea

sun tea

wine

Activities and Traditions of Practice

Bonfires

circle dancing

communion with the faeries

divination

feasting

gathering herbs

handfastings / weddings

rolling wheels (that are set on fire)

staying awake through the entire (short) night from dawn on
    Midsummer Day to the following dawn

torchlight processionals

Acts of Service

Give money or time to a solar energy project

plant trees (especially ones which will provide fruit or berries
to feed birds and wildlife)

volunteer at a food kitchen (feeding those who need help)

volunteer at an animal shelter

Alternate Names for Midsummer in Other Pagan Traditions

Alban Hefin (Modern Druids)

Enyovden (Bulgaria)

Festival or Feast of Baldur/Balder (Norse)

Festival of Jāņi (Latvia)

Feill-Sheathain

Gathering Day

Ivan Kupala Day (Russia, Ukraine, Poland)

Juhannas (Finland)

Litha

Meán Samhraidh (modern Celtic, middle of summer)

St. John's Eve (June 23)

St. John's Day/Feast of St. John/Johnmas (June 24, Christian)

Sankthansaften (Saint John's Eve, Denmark, Norway)

Sonnenwende (Norse/German—Sun's Turning)

Summer Solstice

Sun Blessing

Thing-Tide

Holidays or Traditions Occurring During Midsummer in the Northern Hemisphere:

RELIGIOUS

Vestalia, the Festival of Vesta (Ancient Rome: June 7–15)

Gwyl o Cerridwen (Feast of Cerridwen; modern Welsh
    Witchcraft: July 13)

St. Alban's Day (England, Wales: June 20 or 22)

Golowan (Cornwall: June 20–29) with Mazey Day on Sum-
    mer Soltice

SECULAR

Canada Day (July 1)

Independence Day (USA, July 4)

Bastille Day (France, July 14)

Fête de la Musique (World Music Day June 21)

Holidays or Traditions Occurring During Midsummer in the Southern Hemisphere:

RELIGIOUS

Advent (Christian; date varies, but involves the four Sundays
    before Christmas)

Chalica (First week in December; Unitarian Universalists)

St. Barbara's Day (December 4; Christian)

Sanghamittā Day (Buddhist; First full moon in December;
   Sri Lanka)

Chanukah/Hanukkah (variable date; Jewish)

St. Nicholas' Day (December 6)

Bodhi Day (December 8; Buddha's enlightenment)

Our Lady of Guadalupe (December 12)

St. Lucia's Day (December 13)

Saturnalia (December 17–23; Roman)

Christmas; Twelvetide (Twelve Days of Christmas)

Twelfth Night (January 5)

Epiphany (January 6)

SECULAR

Krampusnacht (Alpine Europe: December 6)

Boxing Day (United Kingdom, Australia, Canada, and New
   Zealand: December 26)

New Year's Eve and New Year's Day (December 31 and
   January 1)

CORRESPONDENCES FOR MIDSUMMER

FURTHER READING

Books

Ardinger, Barbara. *Pagan Every Day: Finding the Extraordinary in Our Ordinary Lives.* San Francisco, CA: Weiser Books, 2006.

Blake, Deborah. *Everyday Witch A to Z: An Amusing, Inspiring & Informative Guide to the Wonderful World of Witchcraft.* Woodbury, MN: Llewellyn, 2008.

———. *The Witch's Broom: The Craft, Lore & Magick of Broomsticks.* Woodbury, MN: Llewellyn, 2014.

———. *The Goddess Is in the Details: Wisdom for the Everyday Witch.* Woodbury, MN: Llewellyn, 2009.

Cunningham, Scott. *Magical Herbalism: The Secret Craft of the Wise.* Woodbury, MN: Llewellyn, 2001.

———. *Wicca: A Guide for the Solitary Practitioner.* Woodbury, MN: Llewellyn, 2002.

Cunningham, Scott, and David Harrington. *The Magical Household: Spells & Rituals for the Home.* Woodbury, MN: Llewellyn, 2002.

Digitalis, Raven. *Planetary Spells & Rituals: Practicing Dark & Light Magick Aligned with the Cosmic Bodies.* Woodbury, MN: Llewellyn, 2010.

Dugan, Ellen. *Cottage Witchery: Natural Magick for Hearth and Home.* Woodbury, MN: Llewellyn, 2005.

———. *Garden Witchery: Magick from the Ground Up.* Woodbury, MN: Llewellyn, 2003.

Dunwich, Gerina. *The Wicca Garden: A Modern Witch's Book of Magickal and Enchanted Herbs and Plants.* New York: Citadel Press, 2001.

Holland, Eileen. *The Wicca Handbook.* London: Weiser Books, 2008.

Jordan, Michael. *Encyclopedia of Gods: Over 2,500 Deities of the World.* New York: Facts on File Inc., 1993.

Kynes, Sandra. *A Year of Ritual: Sabbats & Esbats for Solitaries & Covens.* Woodbury, MN: Llewellyn, 2004

Loar, Julie. *Goddesses for Every Day: Exploring the Wisdom & Power of the Divine Feminine Around the World*. Novato, CA: New World Library, 2008.

Monaghan, Patricia. *The Goddess Path: Myths, Invocations & Rituals*. Woodbury, MN: Llewellyn, 1999.

O'Gaea, Ashleen. *Raising Witches: Teaching the Wiccan Faith to Children*. Pompton Plains, NJ: New Page Books, 2002.

Skye, Michelle. *Goddess Alive! Inviting Celtic & Norse Goddesses into Your Life*. Woodbury, MN: Llewellyn, 2007.

Starhawk, Diane Baker, and Anne Hill. *Circle Round: Raising Children in Goddess Traditions*. New York: Bantam Books, 2000.

West, Kate. *The Real Witches' Year: Spells, Rituals, and Meditations for Every Day of the Year*. Woodbury, MN: Llewellyn, 2008.

Online

PaganSquare (from the publishers of *Witches & Pagans Magazine*): http://witchesandpagans.com/.

Paganism/Wicca from Patti Wigington: http://paganwiccan.about.com/.

BIBLIOGRAPHY

Books

Auset, Priestess Brandi. *The Goddess Guide: Exploring the Attributes and Correspondences of the Divine Feminine.* Woodbury, MN: Llewellyn, 2009.

Blake, Deborah. *Circle, Coven & Grove: A Year of Magickal Practice.* Woodbury, MN: Llewellyn, 2007.

Campanelli, Pauline. *Wheel of the Year: Living the Magical Life.* Woodbury, MN: Llewellyn, 1989.

Carr-Gomm, Philip. *Sacred Places: Sites of Spiritual Pilgrimages from Stonehenge to Santiago de Compostela.* London: Quercus, 2009.

Cole, Jennifer. *Ceremonies of the Seasons: Exploring and Celebrating Nature's Eternal Cycle.* London: Duncan Baird Publishers, 2006.

Cunningham, Scott. *Cunningham's Encyclopedia of Magical Herbs.* Woodbury, MN: Llewellyn, 2000.

Franklin, Anna. *Midsummer: Magical Celebrations of the Summer Solstice.* Woodbury, MN: Llewellyn, 2002.

Johnson, Cait. *Witch in the Kitchen: Magical Cooking for All Seasons.* Rochester, VT: Destiny Books, 2001.

Pritchard, Belsebuub and Angela. *The Path of the Spiritual Sun: Celebrating the Solstices & Equinoxes.* Self-published, 2013.

Starhawk. *The Spiral Dance: A Rebirth of the Ancient Religion of the Great Goddess.* 10th Anniversary Edition. New York: HarperCollins Publishers, 2011.

Wood, Jamie, and Tara Seefeldt. *The Wicca Cookbook: Recipes, Ritual, and Lore.* Berkley, CA: Celestial Arts, 2000.

Online

"7 Strange silly summer traditions," *CNN.com,* accessed February 8, 2014, http://www.cnn.com/2013/06/20/world/strange-silly-summer-traditions/.

"About 'Fête *de la Musique,'*" accessed April 6, 2014, http://www.fetedelamusique.culture.fr/en/International/presentation/.

"Germany, Externsteine," *Sacred Destinations,* accessed February 8, 2014, http://www.sacred-destinations.com/germany/externsteine.

"Golowan," accessed April 6, 2014, http://www.golowan.org/.

"History," Stonehenge.co.uk, accessed August 12, 2014, http://www.stonehenge.co.uk/history.php.

"Solstice and Equinox Traditions," *Spiritual Humanism*, accessed February 2, 2014, http://www.spiritualhumanism.org/solequin.php.

"Solstice in Times Square," *Times Square NY,* accessed February 8, 2014, http://www.timessquarenyc.org/events/solstice-in-times-square/.

"Summer Solstice Traditions," *History Lists*, accessed February 1, 2014, http://www.history.com/news/history-lists/summer-solstice-traditions.

"Sun gods and goddesses," *Ancient/classical History*, accessed February 5, 2014, http://ancienthistory.about.com/od/sungodsgoddesses/a/070809sungods.htm.

"Wianki Krakow—Midsummer Night Celebration," Cracow Online, accessed April 6, 2014, http://www.cracowonline.com/1843-Wianki_Krakow_-_Midsummer_Night_Celebration.html.

.

INDEX

C

Y

About the Author

Deborah Blake is the author of *Circle, Coven and Grove: A Year of Magickal Practice* (Llewellyn 2007), *Everyday Witch A to Z: An Amusing, Inspiring & Informative Guide to the Wonderful World of Witchcraft* (Llewellyn 2008), *The Goddess is in the Details: Wisdom for the Everyday Witch* (Llewellyn 2009), *Everyday Witch A to Z Spellbook* (2010) and *Witchcraft on a Shoestring* (2010). She has published numerous articles in Pagan publications, including Llewellyn annuals and has an ongoing column in *Witches & Pagans* Magazine.

Her award-winning short story, "Dead and (Mostly) Gone" is included in the Pagan Anthology of Short Fiction: 13 Prize Winning Tales (Llewellyn, 2008). Deborah had been interviewed on television, radio and podcast, and can be found online at Facebook, Twitter, and www.myspace.com /deborahblakehps.

When not writing, Deborah runs The Artisans' Guild, a cooperative shop she founded with a friend in 1999, and also works as a jewelry maker. She lives in a 100-year-old farmhouse in rural upstate New York with four cats who supervise all her activities, both magickal and mundane.

Other Books by Deborah Blake

Circle, Coven and Grove: A Year of Magickal Practice

Everyday Witch A to Z

Everyday Witch A to Z Spellbook

Everyday Witch Book of Rituals

The Goddess is in the Details

The Witch's Broom

A Witch's Dozen

Witchcraft on a Shoestring